AF266255

Journey to Your Self

How to Heal from Trauma

Written by Someone Who Did

Sandra Cooze

Serafina Fae Publishing

Journey to Your Self - How to Heal from Trauma
Written by Someone Who Did
Sandra Cooze

First Edition Published February 2021
Second Edition Published November 2024
All rights reserved
Front Cover Photo: Banter Snaps
Author Photo: Brigitte Bourgoin/Brigitte Bourgoin Portraits
Graphic Design: Sandra Cooze
Copyright © 2021 Sandra Cooze

This book may not be reproduced in whole or part, in any
manner whatsoever without written permission, with the
exception of brief quotations within book reviews or articles.

ISBN: 978-1-0690943-1-5
Library and Archives Canada

Publisher Imprint:
Serafina Fae Publishing

For You

May you find the answers you seek within these pages

to release the past and rise above your story.

The Story behind my Publisher Imprint
Serafina Fae Publishing

In 2013, I opened my very first business. I called it 'Serafina Fae'. The name is a combination of the Italian word for Angel and the umbrella term of mystical creatures. I chose this name because it deeply resonated with me and was the perfect combination for what I had to offer: Handcrafted spiritual and healing jewelry, Tarot and Akashic Record Readings, as well as Reiki. It was through this first business of mine that I discovered my passion, purpose, and gift for trauma healing. Then in 2018, *Rise Above Your Story* was born, replacing *Serafina Fae*, as I had evolved beyond its boundaries. However, its name still holds so much meaning for me that I decided to use it as my Publisher Imprint. It is the most fitting way to honor my journey and evolution. And it allows me to take *Serafina Fae* with me wherever I go.

About the Author

 Sandra Cooze is an Intuitive Therapist, Certified Coach, Reiki Master/Teacher, TIR Facilitator, passionate writer, and creator of the 'Divine Ancestral Healing' Method.

Born and raised in Germany until love brought her to Canada, where she, her husband Jim and their son Cedric live in the beautiful island province of Newfoundland. Her unique perspective of trauma guided her to develop a revolutionary healing approach that has already helped countless women and men liberate themselves from their harrowing past and find true joy and happiness in their lives moving forward.

Sandra studied the Art & Science of Coaching at Erickson College International, Reiki Level 1–Master at Beaumont Hospital, and Traumatic Incident Reduction in Windsor, Ontario.

With her Transformational Trilogy Journey to Your Self, Sandra walks her readers not only through her own story of abuse and self-empowerment, but even more so, guides them through the process of releasing their own trauma, limiting beliefs and self-sabotaging behavior in order to discover their own 'true Self'.

Learn more about her at www.riseaboveyourstory.com.

Table of Contents

"The most rewarding Journey you can ever embark on

is the Journey to Your Self."

–Sandra Cooze

Foreword

Life is an evolving journey with many twists and turns. It's easy to lose ourselves along the way, especially if you've experienced trauma. Sandra Cooze understands the turbulent journey firsthand and has made it her mission to help others through theirs. Journey to Your Self gently guides you through the healing process by encouraging you to work through your past and build a better future. Cooze is a Certified Coach and Traumatic Incident Reduction facilitator and shares countless techniques that she uses in her own practice.

"Trauma healing is a journey of transformation, where we slowly break down our protective shields, our limiting beliefs, and self-sabotaging behavior."

The author's life was permanently altered by her sexual assault experiences, yet she was able to adjust her mindset and find a purpose for her pain. Now she is turning those tough memories into guiding lights for other survivors. If you're struggling to find your way, Journey to Your Self is a compassionate, actionable workbook that will set you on the right path.

–Jenn Sadai, Author of Women Ready to Rise, Canadian Book Award Winner

Author's Preface

Dear Reader,

Every book tells a story. Even scientific, non-fiction, and how-to books tell a story. They tell the story of how the writer reached a point of knowledge that he or she felt compelled to share. Some stories are easy to read; others are not. Some stories inspire us; others trigger us. It all greatly depends on your mindset at the time you read that book.

Have you noticed how some books are easy to read, engaging, and fun, while others seem like a manual that puts you to sleep before you reach page three? The reason is simply that you are open to receiving the message of one book but aren't ready to embrace the wisdom of another just yet.

Each person is on a journey. Throughout our lives, we explore and grow. We constantly learn and adjust our mindsets based on the experiences we have and the knowledge we gain.

When you read my book, you will be confronted with my story. The first section is about the trauma I experienced, and the second section will walk you through the key moments of my transformation. Throughout the chapters of this book, I will use examples from my experiences to explain trauma and the behaviors that come from it. Some chapters may trigger you, and some stories will be hard to read.

The reason I choose to be this open and forthcoming about my own experiences is that I want you to see that I truly understand what it means to be traumatized and that I know how it feels to truly let go. I want you to see that I walked the walk before I talked the talk. I also want you to see that I mean it when I say that it is possible for anyone to overcome trauma. And the best way to do that is by picking a traumatic event apart and studying all of the little behavioral patterns that result from it.

Once I began to embrace my past and made the conscious choice to help others on their journey back to themselves, the knowledge that I had gained over the years began to seep into my consciousness. That was the moment my whole life changed. I found my purpose, and it just felt right.

We may not always know why we do the things we do or take the paths we take. But if we are open to believing that these paths have a purpose and will get us to a specific goal, then our choices can never be wrong.

Warm Wishes,
Sandra Cooze

You Are Not Broken

The other day, I received a message from a reader who asked how we would know if we were too damaged to be fixed. This question was so heartbreaking.

All I wanted to do was reach through my screen and hug her fiercely. Instead, I wrote a reply:

"Dear [Name], thank you for your question. When we are stuck in deep trauma, it can seem as if there is no help for us. But that is not true. Whatever happened to us, whatever the story, we can heal from it. It may seem like an impossible task, especially when the pain is so great, but if we have the courage to stand up for ourselves and choose to heal from our trauma, we will find a way. I have learned a lot about trauma and triggers during my healing journey, and I came to find that once I understood what trauma actually is and what it does to our bodies, minds, and spirits, it wasn't all that intimidating anymore."

Over the next few days, I thought about all of those women, men, and children who believe that they are broken and who will live with this perceived brokenness for the rest of their lives. And I knew that I had to find an ironclad way to explain why I believe that trauma does not break us and, most of all, that we can heal. Then I had a major epiphany.

(That's what I love most about being intuitive. A thought, or an image, just pops into your mind, and everything becomes crystal clear.) That day, I created a video for my YouTube channel

@SandraCoozeUnfiltered about a paper cut.

You see, a paper cut is probably one of the least threatening and most annoying wounds we will ever receive. So, in this chapter, I will demonstrate to you how trauma is not much different from a paper cut. I will also demonstrate how, if we approach it in the same way, we can let go of any and all trauma with ease.

So, let's say you just received an envelope in the mail that you had been waiting for weeks to receive, and finally it is here. You can't wait to read what it says. Without hesitation, you just rip it open and...ouch! You get a paper cut right in the crease of your index finger. It hurts, it stings, it bleeds, and it burns. So, what do you do? You hold it under cold running water to clean it and attempt to stop the bleeding. If it is really bad, you may get a Band-Aid. And then what? Nothing. You just move on. The finger is taken care of, and the wound will heal on its own. Am I right?

But what if we looked at it from a different perspective. Because, actually, the moment the paper cut into your finger, your finger became traumatized. It received a wound, and with that it experienced trauma. So why is it that after your finger has been traumatized, you take care of it and move on, never looking back? Why don't you keep going back to the moment the paper cut happened, playing it back in your mind over and over again? Why are you not terrified of ever touching paper or opening an envelope again?

Well, I believe—no, I know—why, as do you. Our bodies are self-healing. And—and here is where it gets interesting—I believe that it does not matter what wounds our bodies, minds, and spirits receive. We can heal from anything. We are self-healing on all levels.

When we are traumatized, it is, in essence, the same as the paper cut. We get attacked, abused, or experience other forms of traumatic events. However, rather than healing our bodies and moving on with our day-to-day business, as we would do after cutting a finger, we continue to circle back to the trauma. We are so focused on what happened that we are literally blocking our bodies from doing what they are supposed to do: heal.

And yet we don't think twice about that paper cut.

Now, you could argue that a traumatic event and a paper cut are not the same thing, and you would be right. It is not the same level of trauma, but for our bodies, this does not matter. Our bodies only know that healing is needed and that they have to do their job. For our bodies, it does not matter if we get a paper cut, break a bone, get a new kidney, or experience trauma. Healing is healing. The difference is our inability to move past what happened. We keep ourselves stuck in the trauma and, because of that, keep ourselves from healing.

In other words, holding on to the incidents that traumatized us is the same as constantly peeling off a scab caused by a paper cut and therefore forcing it to continuously bleed. And that, ladies and gentlemen, is exactly what we are doing when we are holding on to trauma. We are preventing our bodies from doing their job by forcing them to continuously suffer through the trauma over and over again.

If we are able to heal ourselves, then why does it seem so impossible to heal from trauma? Well, first of all, we have been taught that trauma can't be healed, that it can only be lived with. We have been taught that the body heals physical wounds, but I have honestly never heard any doctor tell me that the body also heals mental and emotional wounds. However, what I did hear a lot was that "time heals all wounds." But that is the wrong way of thinking about it, in my opinion. Because time is just time. It can't heal anything. No, time does not heal any wounds; we do. If we believe that time heals all wounds, we focus on the time, not on ourselves. We just wait for time to pass and expect our emotional pain to just vanish one day.

So, instead of saying "time heals all wounds," shift your mindset to yourself and say, "I heal all of my wounds."

But how do we accomplish that? How do we tap into the full capacity of our healing abilities? I see the self-healing ability as a muscle that needs to be exercised in order to increase its mobility, strength, and resilience. We have to massage out all of those knots that formed because our abilities weren't trained enough. We slowly stretch them and allow them to gradually adjust to the new norm.

And with Journey to Your Self—How to Heal from Trauma, I will help you massage out the knots by showing you what aspects of trauma and yourself you will have to release in order to reconnect and realign. I will help you strengthen that muscle that is your self-healing ability and help you teach it to do what it is meant to do: heal on all levels.

Now, with our new mantra, "I heal all my wounds," in mind, let's get started.

About Journey to Your Self

When I decided to write Journey to Your Self— How to Heal from Trauma, I wanted it to be more than just a book. I wanted it to be an inspiration, a guide, and a workbook. I wanted to create a book that not only talks about trauma healing but that also gives you the tools you need to heal your trauma. I did not want to create just another book that only talks about how to overcome trauma; I wanted my book to also incorporate exercises and challenges that can help you begin and continue your healing journey.

Over the past decade, I have gained so much insight into what happens the moment we become traumatized, how our bodies create a protection and defense mechanism, and how this defense mechanism can turn into our worst enemy. I continue to be in awe of how many different aspects there are to trauma healing.

In Journey to Your Self—How to Heal from Trauma, I include insights and approaches from a spiritual perspective. I do understand that this may not be for everyone, and I am not trying to make you firm believers in the "supernatural." I simply ask that you keep an open mind. Many aspects that you see as spiritual are actually a part of who you are and are simultaneously playing a key role in your physical, mental, and emotional body, like your Chakra System.

I will try my best to describe each spiritual aspect in the greatest detail in order to take the "woo-woo" effect out of them.

Every part of this book is meant to support you in your healing journey. Some parts may resonate with you; some may not. And that is perfectly fine. We are each on our own journey. No two are alike. Be open to what you are about to read and give it the benefit of the doubt.

That is all I ask.

How to get the most out of this book

And in a few months' time, you may feel drawn to picking up this book once more and reading it again. And then you may realize that something that hasn't resonated with you before now makes perfect sense, simply because you have evolved and healed parts of yourself and now you are ready for the next step in your journey.

Journey to Your Self - How to Heal from Trauma is meant to grow with you.

As you work through Journey to Your Self—How to Heal from Trauma, you will notice that some chapters have extra space so you can take notes or work through an exercise. Some may make you wonder how they could possibly help you heal from trauma. Allow me to explain. Trauma healing is a journey of transformation where you slowly break down your protective shields, limiting beliefs, and self-sabotaging behavior. This journey's main focus is self-reflection. You can only transform your trauma by taking a good look at yourself and letting go of what holds you back.

Self-reflection can be intimidating, especially when you are afraid of what you may see or how you may feel. The exercises in this book will gently guide you through your maze of thoughts, emotions, feelings, and triggers. Once you realize that observing yourself will allow you to let go of trauma with ease, you will welcome every trigger that comes up.

Once you realize that a trigger is just a guiding light toward what needs to be healed, transformed, and released, you will begin to happily embrace each and every one of them because you'll know that yet another part of your traumatic past is ready to leave.

Trauma healing is all about putting yourself first and fighting for yourself. Healing your trauma means that you must be stronger than your pain. You have to be brave enough to face yourself and embrace the part of you that is hurting, giving it a voice. In order to heal and release your trauma, you have to allow your pain to come forward, embrace it, love that part of you that is in so much agony, and allow it to transform and be released.

If there was one profound realization that I had during my healing journey, it was that **trauma survivors are holding themselves hostage.**

It's time to take back your life.

YOU ARE WORTH FIGHTING FOR!

Have a Pen and Paper Ready

Before you dive into Journey to Your Self—How to Heal from Trauma, I would like to encourage you to get a journal or have a stack of paper and a pen sitting next to you whenever you read. With each chapter, you may feel drawn to reflect on yourself, your journey so far, your breakthroughs, and your setbacks.

Whatever pops into your head, write it down. Even if it is something you forgot to put on your grocery list, write it down. Get it out of your head and onto the paper. This is an incredible form of release. There will be moments when you find yourself filling page after page with thoughts that just flood out of you. When this happens, go with it. This is the moment when you are breaking through emotional blockages, and by writing it all down, you are releasing them for good.

Imagine that your thoughts look like a yarn ball that is rolled up in your mind. The ball could be red, green, or even rainbow. The end of that yarn ball is beginning to untangle and slowly move from your mind, going down your neck, into your shoulder, and down to the arm you hold the pen with. See that string moving down your arm, into your hand, and into the pen. See the yarn flowing out of the pen with every word you write.

Now see how the yarn ball in your mind slowly unravels and becomes smaller and smaller, until every bit of that yarn ball has moved through your neck, into your shoulder, down your arm, through your hand, and out through your pen.

When you put your thoughts to paper, you release their energy. This method is a very powerful way to bring clarity and healing. You don't have to focus on what you write you can just let your hand and pen do the work. It is very important, though, that you do write with your hand. Typing away at the computer won't give you the same energetic release.

Journaling is a very effective way of releasing negative emotions and trauma. Some of you may become scared by the words and phrases you put on paper, because for some who have experienced extreme trauma, very dark or destructive thoughts may come to the surface. To whomever experiences this, please do not be afraid. The thoughts that come up and onto paper are coming up to be <u>released</u>.

These thoughts were buried within you for so long, and now you allow them to come forward. They have to come up to leave your body, mind, and spirit, just as you would have to walk out the door to leave from somewhere. The part that comes up is the part that has been hurting for such a long time. Don't fear that part of you and don't judge it. Give it a voice. It has been suppressed long enough and should be set free.

Often, you probably blame yourself for your trauma or feel that you should have done more. At some point, the blame becomes so great that the only way to live a somewhat normal life is to suppress those emotions. And yet, with every year those emotions are suppressed, they become louder and louder.

Guilt is one of the hardest emotions to deal with because you feel undeserving of forgiveness, even if the person you feel guilty toward has long forgiven you or if there just never was anything to forgive. You may have witnessed something horrifying as a child and were unable to help. You may have witnessed something as an adult and froze up, unable to step in. In cases like these, guilt and shame can become your emotional torturer and executioner.

Another aspect of feeling guilt and shame is that you are the one person you can never get away from. You can torture yourself for the rest of your life, suffering at your own hands simply because you are not allowing yourself to let it go.

However, you are deserving of forgiveness. It is so much easier to forgive someone else for what they have done than to forgive yourself. And yet you are just as deserving of love, compassion, forgiveness, emotional freedom, and peace as anyone else. Healing means forgiving and loving every part of yourself.

Your thoughts, your trauma, your guilt, and your shame are not who you are. They just bury your true self beneath all of the pain.

As you can see, this type of journaling differs greatly from keeping a diary. Journaling is a spiritual practice—spiritual in the sense that it can help release the disruptive energy within you. Technically, it is not even a spiritual practice; rather, it is a psycho-logical approach.

Once you get the hang of it, it is important that you do it with intent.

When you begin to journal, set an intention like this one:

"I am using this pen as a tool to bring to the surface what needs to be released. I allow it to come to the surface, and I embrace, with love and compassion, any word, emotion, or memory that is ready to be seen, heard, felt, and acknowledged. I will not be scared of, discouraged by, or resentful toward the memories, emotions, or thoughts that reveal themselves to me. Instead, I will embrace and love them and allow them to leave."

I would also encourage you to write down a-ha moments you experience while working through this book, and then see what they lead you to release.

Why not make journaling fun by using a special pen, maybe one with a huge feather or one that sparkles all over? Journaling is all about transformation, so use items that inspire you or make you feel happy or peaceful.

Here is a quick summary of how to journal:

1. Get a pen and a piece of paper or a notebook.

2. Make sure you are undisturbed and have some time to yourself. Thirty minutes would be ideal, but it is okay if you don't have that much time.

3. Set the pen on the paper and take a deep breath.

4. Write down the first thing that pops into your head no matter what comes up or how silly you think it is.

5. Let your thoughts flow onto the paper and don't focus too much on them. Just let it happen automatically. It will get easier with time and practice.

6. When you are done, it is up to you whether you read what you wrote or not. I would not suggest keeping the paper. Shred it, burn it, or bury it. Imagine that by doing so, you release the energy of what you just allowed to come to the surface.

7. When you feel overwhelmed by what comes to the surface, put your pen down for a moment. Take a deep breath and release the pressure that is building up within you.

8. Imagine the thoughts that haunt you as energy that is moving about in your body.

9. With each breath in, collect the energy in your core. And with each breath out, push the energy down your torso, into your legs, through your feet, and out into the ground.

10. Repeat until you feel calmer and more balanced.

11. Now shift your focus to the center of your being, which lies in the center of your body, right behind your navel. Envision a ball of golden light that sits at your center. This golden light is your Chi, your Life Force Energy. Feel this light and experience the love and compassion that is the very core of who you are.

12. Focus on that, see the golden ball of light, and see that light radiating outward and filling your entire body with peace, love, and tranquility.

NOW TAKE YOUR PEN AND
BEGIN TO WRITE!

21-day Transformation

You know how the saying goes: "Do something for 21-days, and it becomes a habit." As you work through Journey to Your Self—How to Heal from Trauma and you come across the various exercises, feel free to pick one that you feel drawn to and practice it for twenty-one days. Use the lines below, or keep a journal to write down your experiences, and at the end of these twenty-one days, reflect on what has changed.

21-day challenge subject: ______________________________

Day 1:

____

____

____

____

____

____

____

____

____

____

____

Day 2:

Day 3:

Day 4:

Day 5:

Day 6:

Day 7:

Day 8:

Day 9:

Day 10:

Day 11:

Day 12:

Day 13:

Day 14:

Day 15:

____
____
____
____
____
____
____
____
____
____
____
____
____
____
____
____

Day 16:

____
____
____
____
____
____
____
____
____

Day 17:

Day 18:

Day 19:

Day 20:

Day 21:

Final self-analysis after the 21-day challenge:

"and here you are living despite it all"

—Rupi Kaur

My Story

I grew up in a loving family. My family was not rich or wealthy, but we had good lives. Just like any other twelve-year-old girl, I had a dream. I wanted to ride. I was in love with horses and dreamed of having my own someday.

One day, my mother made my dream come true. She was not able to buy me a horse or pay for riding lessons, but she had a friend who had a stable and was looking for someone who could take care of her little pony. To say I was over-the-moon excited would have been an understatement! This opportunity meant the world to me.

Every Tuesday and Thursday afternoon, I would come home from school, eat lunch, and then take the bus to the stables. (My mother would pick me up most days after work.)

There was an older man, maybe in his sixties, who took care of the stables and the horses. He showed me how to saddle a horse, how to brush it, how to scrape its hooves, and, of course, how not to get bitten or kicked while doing all of that.

As much as I enjoyed taking care of that pony, I was in love with the big horses, so when the stable master one day asked me if I wanted to ride on his horse to get a feel for being on a big one, I was more than willing to go.

I climbed up onto this beautiful golden-brown animal, and the stable master held the reins and walked beside us. It was a beautiful, warm summer's day. The air smelled like dust, flowers, grass, and horse.

We walked beside fenced meadows and a couple of fields until we came to a shed. He told me that he just had to go inside to get something and that he wanted to give his horse a rest since it was such a warm day. He helped me down, and we went inside.

The shed looked like a small tool shed, and there was saddle equipment everywhere. There were tools hanging on the wall behind a dusty old work bench, and there was a chair that had seen better days as well as a daybed that had a rough blanket on it. It was on that bed where the stable master asked me to sit down. He rummaged around at the other side of the hut and then came over to sit beside me.

He started a conversation with me, asking if I had a boyfriend. Shyly, I said yes, though I found that question to be strange. Then he asked me if my boyfriend had ever kissed me before, and I replied, "Yes, on my cheek."

This man then wrapped his arm around my shoulder, pulled me closer, and kissed me on the cheek.

What happened next startled me and made me become as stiff as a statue. His hand—the one that was holding me by the shoulder—moved under my arm, seemingly to hold me by the waist, but instead it moved up and came to rest on my left breast. He began to stroke me gently and continued to kiss me on the cheek. At the same time, he placed his other hand on my knee and moved it slowly up my leg.

I did not understand what he was doing or why he had suddenly started breathing more heavily. All the while, he was stroking my breast and moving his hand up my leg, getting closer and closer to a part I instinctively knew I did not want to have touched. But I was too mortified to react.

I gathered all my courage and asked, "Shouldn't we go back?" The man breathed in response, "Not yet." So, I endured the molestation for what seemed to be an eternity.

When I came home from the stables that day, I did not know what to do. I did not know if I should tell anyone. I felt strange. I was worried that my parents would be angry or disappointed in me. I could not make sense of what had happened. Luckily, I had told a friend who came by that day, and he insisted that I tell my parents. He even went with me to my mom, who thankfully believed me and took me out of that situation immediately. But that is not where this story ends. When I told my mother, her first and only words were "Don't go there anymore," and this incident was never mentioned again. No explanation of what had happened. No emotional support.

Nothing could have prepared my mother for what I told her that day. I sometimes think about how many thoughts must have rushed through her head. How guilty she must have felt for putting me in this situation, though it was not her fault. She could not have known. No one could have known. She did what she thought was best in this situation. She made an executive decision based on her own mindset and upbringing. She hoped that by not mentioning this incident again and by not pressing charges, I would eventually forget it ever happened, and at first I did forget, but I was going to remember all of it when I was sixteen and old enough to understand exactly what had happened to me.

Fast forward two years in the future. Like every year for as long as I can remember, my family and I went on vacation to Austria. We always went to the same place. It was a family tradition that my grandparents had started. We always went to a hotel high up in the mountains of Tirol, near Salzburg, the birthplace of Wolfgang Amadeus Mozart.

It was a trip the whole family always looked forward to. Mountains everywhere, fresh air, and amazing food. We had been traveling to this beautiful place for so many years that the owners of the hotel considered us family.

The owner liked to drink. A lot. He had developed an ongoing habit of drinking welcome shots with the hotel guests. And since the restaurant was always full and the hotel always booked solid, you can imagine how drunk he eventually became. Drinking wasn't the only bad habit he practiced, though. He was also known for teasingly groping women's breasts. Most female guests knew this about him and endured his advances simply because no one felt there was any ulterior motive behind his casually inappropriate advances. He was, more often than not, seen as the drunken hotel owner who simply liked to fondle women's breasts. His vice was no secret, and no one ever really complained about him, mostly because he never did anything more than that.

One day during this fateful vacation in 1988, my parents left me and my sister under the hotel owner's supervision for about half an hour to inspect new accommodations that were being built for guests.

I would have never expected the owner to come at me that day and actually try to touch my breasts. I was, after all, only fourteen years old. Still an innocent, but not naïve. I immediately yelled "NO," then ran away from him. But my voice was not heard. No matter how many times I said no, my feelings didn't matter. He just kept coming after me, practically chasing me around the hotel. It seemed as if it was a game for him. He was amused by my efforts to escape him. This traumatic ordeal went on for about half an hour until my parents finally returned.

I ran to my mother, tears in my eyes, and told her what had happened. To my dismay, my feelings were dismissed. My mother decided to laugh off the entire ordeal and explained to me that the owner did that to every woman and that he meant no harm. Then, in a joking tone, she told the owner that he couldn't behave inappropriately with her fourteen-year-old daughter since she did not understand that he was just playing around. I was stunned into silence and grief. I felt as though my mother had failed me. She had made me feel like a silly, naïve girl for not allowing this lecher to touch my breasts.

What I ended up learning that day was this: Not only was it common, but it was also completely accepted that a man could touch a woman wherever he wanted, whenever he pleased. Women had no say in the matter. This day ended up being the last time I confided in my parents about any serious matter.

When I was sixteen years old, I had a class in school that covered sexual assault and where to seek help should this happen. Up to this point, I had buried the memories of the previous two assaults deep within my soul. But that day when we had this class, everything just flooded back into my consciousness, and this time I understood. I knew exactly what had happened. And that made it even worse. I remembered the touching, the stroking, and the chasing, and I remembered that my parents had not protected me.

About six months later, the bullying started in school. It went on for about a year. My classmates would tease and kick me during breaks, usually while I was sitting by myself, buried in a book. They would shoot spitballs at me. They bullied away the only friend I had at school. They intentionally forced me into isolation.

One day, I was writing a letter to my pen pal, telling her about having a boyfriend and how happy I was. That letter was stolen from my backpack by my classmates, and copies of it were distributed throughout the entire school. I felt so humiliated.

One day, I confided in my grandma about the bullying, and she told me to just ignore my classmates and assured me that they would eventually stop. But they didn't. Only when the teacher finally stepped in would they leave me be. But I never told my parents one word about any of this. I had learned, yet again, that nothing would come from confiding in my family. Eventually, the bullying stopped, but not before they destroyed my ability to trust anyone. It took me a long time to overcome this distrust and allow people close again.

Born and raised in Germany, I had had the luxury of a fully paid education and the choice of a trade or profession. When I was nineteen years old, I chose hotel business because I was drawn to the hospitality industry. I had dreamed of working on a cruise ship and traveling the world, or even running a hotel, someday. But life had other plans.

While completing my education in a large exhibition hotel, I was assigned to work a few months in every department. Housekeeping was my favorite part. I loved helping people and straightening out the rooms with the maids. I felt as if I was making a difference in people's lives.

During my time in housekeeping, a cleaning service was hired to help the maids with the workload during the busy exhibition season. I was always nice and respectful to everyone, including the crew of the cleaning service, which was all men. I smiled at them when I saw them and went about my business. One of the men took my smiles as an invitation to pursue me. He came at me, touched my hand, and tried to kiss me. Already confused and carrying trauma, this shocked me deeply, and I began to question how I was supposed to communicate with men without sending the wrong signals.

Eventually, I transferred to the restaurant to learn all about meal preparation and service. The restaurant was leased by an Italian, and most of his employees were Italian, as well. It was while working in this restaurant that I experienced the most disrespectful, chauvinistic, and inappropriate sexual harassment of my life. The employees had no sense of personal boundaries, decency, or respect for privacy. There were many instances when servers would just walk into changing rooms that had no privacy locks. Several times, I was embarrassed and humiliated by employees who knew full well that I was changing yet blatantly disregarded my need for privacy. There was one waiter in particular who, even when I asked him to leave, would purposely invade my personal space and disregard my protests. He would just stand there, arms crossed, leaning against an armoire and watching me with a smirk on his face knowing full well what he did was wrong, but enjoying it regardless. Another time, I was in the ladies' room, and that same waiter came into the bathroom and handed me the phone underneath the bathroom stall because my mother had called.

I couldn't believe the appalling behavior that went on in this restaurant and could not wait for my training there to end. No matter where I worked in this restaurant, I always felt very demeaned, insecure, and incredibly stressed among those employees. I was always on guard, looking over my shoulder.

I never told anyone about this sexual harassment because I didn't believe anything would change if I reported it. Past experiences had taught me that I would not get any help, anyway. I realized with each year that passed that experiences like this made me feel deeply insignificant and worthless as a woman.

Despite everything, I was a romantic soul. I dreamed of finding my prince charming, who would whisk me away on a white horse and love me for who I was. So, one evening in my early twenties, I went on a first date with a young man. We went to the local Irish pub and enjoyed a meal together. A woman who had roses in her arms came into the pub, and the young man bought one for me.

I thought it was the sweetest thing until he took my hand not five minutes later and placed it on his crotch. I immediately pulled my hand away in disgust and wanted to leave. However, he profusely apologized and asked me to stay. I felt very uncomfortable but chose not to leave because I had been taught that such behavior would be disrespectful. Sadly, I was not taught that it would be perfectly appropriate to leave if my date did something as appalling as this.

When I was twenty-two, I met Roni. We met through a blind date arranged by a couple of my friends and felt an instant connection with one another. We had a good time together. Sometimes his friend Manuel would join us. Both friends were officers in the US Army. Roni, Manuel, and I hung out almost every weekend. We would often go out to different clubs or have game nights at one of the guys' places. It was always a fun time.

One night, we were at Manuel's place and had a bit too much to drink. Roni went home since he had to get up for work early the next day. I decided to stay and sober up before driving home myself, as I lived about thirty minutes away.

Manuel suggested that I sleep over since I had been drinking; plus, the roads were icy and slippery that January winter evening. I agreed and decided to stay. We had known each other for a few months, and there was no reason not to trust him.

I made myself comfortable and decided to go to sleep in the huge king-size bed. There was plenty of space for us to sleep far apart. Five people could have fit in between us easily. I was fully clothed in a t-shirt and some sweatpants, and I was drifting off to sleep on my side of the bed when suddenly I felt him next to me, touching my breasts.

I immediately told him to stop and pushed his hand away. But he kept on pursuing me as I continued to resist and reject his unwelcome sexual advances. I was mortified, in shock, unprepared for this disturbing pass made upon my body. He had never shown any interest in me before, and I didn't know how to make him stop groping me. I was so afraid and, at the same time, disgusted by the feeling of his hands touching me against my will.

Eventually, he realized how upset I was and stopped. But by then, I was very afraid and worried he would try again. I didn't know what to do and didn't know whether to trust him. I couldn't leave because I was afraid that I was still too tipsy to drive on slippery roads. And I also didn't feel right about waking up Roni, knowing how early he had to get up.

So, I took a deep breath and tried to calm and relax myself. I told myself that I would be okay. After a few minutes, I began to get angry and sarcastically muttered to Manuel, "Can I go to sleep now, or are you going to make a pass at me again?" I thought that my anger and sarcasm would be apparent and understood, yet that was not the case. He instantly misinterpreted my flippant remark as an invitation and jumped me.

Before I could even protest, he tugged my sweats down and threw himself on top of me. I was mortified when he entered me. Somehow, I found the strength to throw him off. I have no idea where that strength came from because he literally flew across the room. It was in that sober moment that he finally snapped out of his dazed drunkenness.

I jumped off the bed, wrapped myself in a blanket, and began screaming the word "rape" at him. I was frantic, in a panicked rage, trying to get dressed and leave his place as quickly as I could. I kept watching to make sure Manuel wasn't anywhere near me. I kept asking myself how he could have misinterpreted my words. I realized then that I should never mock or berate a drunk, aroused man.

I ran to Roni's apartment and told him about Manuel's unwanted assault on me. I expected Roni to stand up for me, especially since Manuel had clearly crossed boundaries with both his girlfriend and his good friend. But Roni did nothing. I was shocked and terribly hurt by his response. "Manuel is my friend. And I won't jeopardize my friendship with him over this." I just stood there in total disbelief. The one person who was supposed to care for me and protect me just brushed my experience off as if it was nothing. Needless to say, I left feeling like an object that could be used and then disposed of.

When I walked into my home the night after the assault, my father was still awake. He looked at me and must have seen how distressed I was. And at that moment, he understood what had happened. I didn't know how he knew, but he took one look at my face that day and said, "He tried, didn't he?" I just shook my head and said, "No, he actually did it." My dad just nodded, and I turned away to go to my bedroom, where I could be alone.

When I emerged from my room later that day, rested and calmed, my father informed me that Manuel had called several times and that he had told him I wasn't home. Yet he also said that he could not keep doing this and that I should talk to him. So, the next time Manuel called, I answered the phone. He had called because he was worried that I would report him, of course. But I half-heartedly assured him that I wouldn't do that and hung up the phone. I never heard from him or saw him again.

It was after that sexual assault that I began to question and doubt myself. I began to look for reasons why this had happened to me again. Why had I attracted this horrible experience? Did I not know how to read men? Did Manuel flirt with me at some point, and did I not notice? Or did I simply misinterpret his communication with me? Was I too open and free in my communication with him? Where had I led this guy on? So many questions passed through my mind, all of them self-interrogating, almost self-incriminating.

This is what many victims of sexual assault and abuse do. They look for reasons to blame themselves because they think it's the only plausible reason why someone would assault them.

No matter how many questions I asked, I realized that I was not getting anywhere with this self-interrogation, so I decided to confide in my friends and report this guy to the military police. And yet again, I was faced with dismissal. My friends laughed my intentions off, acting as if I was ridiculous, and predicted that I would not be vindicated and that nothing at all would be resolved by my accusing a military man of rape. Instead, they said I should tell them that I had a relationship with him and had found out that he had a wife in the USA. This, they said, would spark the MP's interest, as they held marriages in very high regard.

Needless to say, I did not go to the police, because I was quite discouraged by their advice and disturbed by their suggestion for me to lie to the officials about Manuel. Eventually, I sought my dad's opinion about going to the MP, and he flat-out said to me, "It is you against the entire US Army. Who do you think is going to win?" So, I dropped my desire to press charges and never again pursued the incident.

My decision to forget the sexual assault happened made me further withdraw from life. I stopped going out. I stopped seeing my friends. I felt no desire to dance. I felt no desire to socialize. I felt nothing but fear, anxiety, and emptiness. I became more and more overwhelmed by this great need to isolate myself and search for a way to heal my violated mind and body. This sexual assault ended up haunting me for years.

To this day, I still remember how I felt hours after Manuel raped me. Every memory of that night would remind me of the stable master's hands on my young body. I couldn't escape all of the memories, the disturbing images, and the feelings that would arise every time I thought of the men who had violated me physically and emotionally. You never forget that desperation. You never forget that kind of fear and trauma. It goes deep into the heart, deep into your very cells. And all it took to trigger those disturbing memories was a simple dismissal, rejection, or attack on my feelings.

About a year after Manuel raped me, I decided to go out with my friends. I had pushed my trauma into the depth of my mind and had begun to feel better about myself and the world around me. We went to a newly opened Cuban club. I loved the music and was excited to go. I was asked to dance by a young Cuban man. We danced to swift Cuban tunes. But of course, my bliss did not last long. My dance partner pushed his torso against mine and held me very tight. I could feel his growing erection rubbing against my crotch. I desperately tried to push him away, but he would not let go of me, instead pressing even harder against me. I felt sick to my stomach, disgusted, and helpless. My friends said they saw what happened, yet not one of them stepped in. They just asked why I did not push him away.

That was the last time I ever went dancing.

A year after this last incident, I decided to seek professional help. I did not like the person I had become and wanted to free myself from this burden. All I wanted was a happy life. Yet the past held me hostage.

My family doctor was very kind and compassionate, and referred me to a psychologist, where I spent an hour talking about all of the things that had happened and my life in general. At the end of our session, he looked at me and said, "I believe you have already worked through it all. What am I supposed to do?"

I could not believe what I had been told. I had been dismissed yet again. My feelings were not heard; my pain was not being taken seriously. All I felt was defeat. "I give up!" I exclaimed. I went home that day wondering why I had been punished in this way. What had I ever done to the world to deserve such treatment?

Sometimes we have to hit rock bottom in order to find our way back up again. And I had just hit rock bottom.

My Journey to My Self

I wish I could tell you that I had this incredible moment of profound clarity or that I had a visit from my guardian angel, who took me by the hand and guided me through my pain and into the light, causing my trauma to just fall off of me like a worn-out blanket. But I can't. Just like everyone else, I had to challenge myself to get through the tough stuff.

The deeper I reflected on my life, the more I felt like everything I deserved had been taken from me: my innocence, my self-confidence, my trust, my freedom, and my carefree, fun-loving nature. All of these important qualities were stolen from me. My joys and my love for dancing and horseback riding. All of the sacred passions of my youth were doused by the uncontrollable urges of adult men who were clearly unconscious of how wrong and disturbing their assaults were.

When I was depressed, I felt like I would never get back my life, much less awaken to the joys of living again. I couldn't even imagine truly enjoying the things I once loved. I always feared I would remember the buried trauma and the ugly, disturbing memories. I couldn't go to a stable or even see a horse without thinking about being molested as a child. I couldn't go to a hotel or resort without remembering being chased by a madman who wanted to grope a fourteen-year-old's breasts. I couldn't walk by men without having a deep fear and distrust of them. These dark, haunting memories followed me everywhere I went for many years.

I convinced myself that I would never really escape this trauma. I existed, barely surviving, only going where I had to go and talking to who I had to talk to. And sadly, years passed before I learned that we should never allow ourselves to be defined or overpowered by our past experiences. Years passed before I was finally able to move through and past my trauma. Because I didn't know how to deal with the blows life had dealt me, I had given up on life. I had given up on any hope of being truly happy and free of my dark past. Instead, I suppressed all of the pain, all of the memories, and all of the anger, disappointment, and sorrow. I even suppressed my hope of finding someone who would understand my pain and help me. I had completely given up on everyone, including myself.

But we all know that any denial or suppression of our true feelings is an act of self-betrayal and self-sabotage that eventually comes back to either haunt us or resurrect us. Denial and suppression never help. If anything, they cause increasingly greater pain, fear, anxiety, and depression. Eventually, the pain becomes so overwhelming that the trauma can no longer be ignored.

And this becomes the defining moment when we experience the darkest pain of our lives, the moment mystics call the dark night of the soul. Such a harrowing experience will either make us or break us. Some souls decide they can't go on and leave the planet in desperation; others decide to rise like the phoenix from the ashes of their painful experiences, and they become renewed, reborn into a new being.

As I am reminiscing on the darkest times of my life and the moment my life began to change, two very distinct memories come to mind. The first one taught me to have faith even if I don't understand, and the second one taught me the importance of self-observation.

A couple of months or so after I went to see the psychologist, I had a visit from a good friend named Heiko. He was very spiritual and knowledgeable about how to work with the energies. That fateful day, he saw how miserable I felt. I remember this moment as if it were yesterday. He stood in front of me while I was sitting on my living room couch, looked at me with a stern face, put his hands on his hips, and then raised one hand and waved it around theatrically, saying, "Get a quartz crystal already!"

That memory always brings a smile to my face. He seemed so sincere, and I had no idea what he was talking about. I had never heard of energy or vibration before and had no knowledge about crystals other than the fact that they were pretty.

The following Saturday, we went to a huge flea market that stretched for miles along the river Main in Frankfurt, Germany. Once there, we looked for a vendor that sold crystals, and Heiko guided me to pick out my first quartz crystal. He told me to look for one that felt comfortable in my hand and that either felt warm immediately or tingled. I picked up a crystal that I felt drawn to and held it in my hand. The more I held it, the more I realized that I could not put it down. (This is a common phenomenon with crystals. When you find one that you are supposed to keep, you will not be able to take it out of your hand.)

After I bought the crystal, I still had no idea what to do with it. Heiko told me to cleanse it under running water. He explained that this would clear the energy of other people who may have touched it. He also told me that from then on, I should be the only one to touch it. If another person picked it up, I would have to cleanse it again.

He further explained that the quartz crystal was also called "the poor man's diamond" because its energetic attribute was as valuable as the monetary value of a cut diamond.

The first night I took the quartz crystal to bed with me, I did not know what to expect. According to Heiko's directions, I was supposed to hold the stone in my hand and meditate. I did what he asked to the best of my ability, as I did not really know what meditation meant. So I lay in bed, crystal in my left hand—it felt the most comfortable in this one—and waited. Nothing happened. The second and third night were the same. Nothing except for the crystal getting warm, which was bound to happen since I kept holding it.

But then on the fourth night, I began to feel something. I felt a twirling in the palm of the hand that held the crystal. I could literally feel a circling motion. Today, of course, I know that it was the hand Chakra that had been activated, but back then I was just dumbfounded.

I kept on holding the crystal in my hand every night. On some nights, I felt the twirling; on others, I could not tell where my hand ended and the crystal began. It felt as if the two had fused together. Other nights, I could feel how energy was moving down my arm in a constant stream and, shortly after, pushing up into my arm.

I used the crystal almost every night for three months. At first, I did not notice any changes, but one day something happened. I was at a dance recital and was asked to take a picture of the group. I stood up, and with a loud, clear voice—so everyone could hear me on stage—I guided them to the spots they needed to go to. I had never been a person who would speak up or give firm directions, and the ladies I took the picture of were positively surprised at my transformation. They had known me since I was a teenager and had never seen me like this. That was new! It may not seem like much, but for me that was a huge transformation.

About three years later, after quite a few failed relationships and setbacks, I had a boyfriend who unintentionally gave me the next piece of the puzzle. We had been seeing each other for about two months before it all fell apart. I remember that all I ever wanted was to be loved and to finally find the one who would just marry me so that I would not have to continue looking for Mr. Right anymore. Yet, at the same time, I was sabotaging each and every relationship due to lack of self-esteem, feeling unworthy, and fear of rejection. It was a constant vicious cycle, but until that one fateful day, I didn't realize it.

That day when we broke up, he said, "I have just been married to a woman with mental issues. I do not want another one in my life!" He did not spit it out. He said it a matter of fact way. And those words truly made me think. For the first time, I looked at my behavior and what it had done to my relationships. I began to analyze my actions, thoughts, and feelings. That was a huge turning point because at that moment, I decided that I did not want to be that woman anymore. I decided to stop dating until I felt comfortable with who I was. I realized that it was not about finding the right one; it was about being the right one for myself.

Well, that conscious choice must have been a huge turning point in my journey to My Self, because three months later I met my husband, with whom I just celebrated 20 years of marriage. But that's a whole other story.

Healing trauma is seldom a groundbreakingly huge moment. Instead, it's usually little things that make us go "hmm" and reflect. These two incidences were significant moments in my healing journey. They basically set the foundation for my transformation.

I weaved all of the other key moments and revelations into some of the following chapters.

"The secret of change is to focus all of your energy,

not on fighting the old, but on building the new."

-Dan Millman
"A Book that Changes Lives"

The Three Stages of Trauma

With trauma and the healing process, there are three different stages. The first stage is the "victim stage." The second stage is the "survivor stage," and the third stage is the "thriver stage." In this chapter, I will talk about these three stages, their significance, their purpose, and, of course, how you will know that you are ready to truly heal and let go.

The "victim stage" is the stage you are in right after the traumatizing incident. In this stage, you may feel anxious, scared, terrified, overwhelmed, and, in really bad cases, suicidal. This is also the stage where you try to make sense of what happened, and you usually come to the conclusion that it must have been your fault...because nothing else would make any sense. In this stage, the idea of healing your trauma would terrify you. You would feel anxious, sick to your stomach, and you would run for the hills if anyone so much as suggested that you should heal.

But how long does this stage last? Well, to be honest, it can last for a very long time. It all depends on your ability and willingness to work through the trauma and get to the next stage. However, many trauma survivors who are stuck in this stage do feel that they need help and look for ways to achieve healing. What happens then is that they find someone who can help them, but once a course of action or a treatment plan has been suggested, they retract because the anxiety and fear is still too great. The issue here is that these people may now begin to punish themselves for their weakness. This can cause two very different outcomes:

1. It can draw them further back into the victim mentality, only this time they are also mentally and emotionally abusing themselves with negative self-talk.
2. They get so angry at themselves and their perceived weaknesses that they catapult themselves right into the second, or even last, stage.

Retracting back into the victim stage does not mean that a person can't still heal; it just means that that person has to be tougher than his or her trauma. If you feel that you are stuck in this stage, don't worry. Simply by reading about the different stages and understanding what is happening within you, you may experience major shifts into the next or last stage pretty quickly. Knowledge is power, and once you understand the cause and effect of your mental and emotional state, you have the tools to become empowered and to rise above.

In the "survivor stage," you move past the terror, the fear, and, for the most part, the anxiety, though you may still get really anxious if you are triggered.

In the survivor stage, you are able to distance yourself from your trauma so much that you can look at it from a different point of view. In this stage, you are angry. You are so angry at everything that happened to you, everything you had to endure, and, of course, the people responsible. This also means that you begin to rise above your trauma. Yet, at the root of this anger is grief. You mourn. You mourn the person you used to be. You mourn what you perceive to have lost or what you had stolen from you, like your innocence, joy, and carefree nature. You mourn the person you could have become had that not happened to you.

This stage can also last for a very long time. Many survivors refuse to let go of the anger simply because they refuse to move on. In their minds, forgiveness and healing, as well as accepting what happened, are things they have no control over and are signs of weakness. The thing is, when you are angry, you are not just angry at your attacker or the situation; you are also angry at yourself. You are angry for allowing it to happen, you are angry for not heeding advice, and you are angry for your weakness and your level of stress and anxiety. Essentially, you don't punish your attackers; you punish yourself.

The good thing about this stage is that you are able to put some distance between your past and your present. The trauma is still a part of you, and you are still held hostage by it, but you experience it differently. This stage may give you a false feeling of safety from your past. In this stage, you've successfully suppressed your memories and emotions. Yet this stage can also be dangerous because at any time, you can get triggered and, with that, get catapulted right back into the victim stage.

After the "survivor stage" comes the "thriver stage." This is the stage when you are ready to truly heal and let go of your trauma. In this stage, you have had it with your trauma, your limiting beliefs, and your self-sabotaging behavior that resulted from the trauma. They are hindering you. You have hopes, and you have dreams, but you are in your own way. You self-sabotage and know you are doing it. And yet you don't know how to stop.

In this stage, you are no longer angry; instead, you are rather annoyed with your past. You want it gone, you want your life back, and you want to thrive. This is the stage where you are no longer afraid to look for a way to heal. You just want to be free. You have risen above your pain, your anger, and your grief and are ready to conquer the world.

As great as this stage sounds, though, you still get triggered, you still have flashbacks, and you still feel stuck. It sounds a lot like the "survivor stage." The one significant difference is that you no longer want to feel the way you feel.

This stage can also last for a very long time because in this stage, you have to be open to looking at yourself and your behavior. Trauma healing is all about self-reflection and transformation. You have to understand that the story will not change. It happened, and that will remain that way. You have to understand that healing means allowing yourself to let go and release your attachment to the past. You have to understand that all this time, you were holding yourself hostage, and you have to be okay with that and love that part of yourself regardless of how long you remained imprisoned in your own body, mind, and spirit.

As you can see, each stage has significance in your journey, but it is very important that you don't get stuck in any stage for too long. Throughout this book, I will come back to the different stages in various ways, and I hope that this chapter has shed some light on the journey you have to take, and most of all, I hope you will be ready for it.

Trauma is Not Just the Big Stuff

When you think about trauma, you probably automatically think about something huge, something terrifying, something life altering. But trauma is not just a situation that can alter the course of your life; it can also be something small, something you would not even see as trauma.

Aside from being a life-altering situation, trauma can be anything that changes your perception of yourself to a limiting, degrading one. You are literally being manipulated into dimming your light. You begin to believe that you are less than you truly are. You begin to see yourself as others want you to see yourself. Often, the people who make you dim your light don't even realize they are doing it.

Trauma is not just the big stuff; it is also the little things. Anything that makes you feel less than adequate about something is considered trauma. You may now reflect on a moment in your past. You say that this situation was not traumatizing; it was just a misunderstanding or a bad choice of words. And you may be right. Yet why do you still feel so hurt, disrespected, or agitated about it? If it were just a silly situation, it would not bother you anymore. But whenever something similar happens, you get triggered. A trigger is a response to a traumatic memory that has been brought back into your consciousness by something that made you feel similar emotions.

Don't disregard the small stuff. Whether it is big or small, trauma is trauma. It alters your perception of yourself, and it makes you see the world around you as a very dark and dingy place. If you were not traumatized, you would not feel worthless, stupid, and inadequate. Trauma is trauma.

No trauma is worth holding on to. No matter what happened, you can choose to transform and heal.

Disillusionment And Self-Preservation

Sexual assault victims often say that their attacker took something from them. Yet if we ask them to explain what they mean, they would usually struggle for words to express exactly how they feel.

When you are being assaulted or abused, first you are in shock, because you did not see it coming. Then the shock is followed by disbelief because what was done to you in any shape or form was done to you against your will. And lastly, you go into survival mode. And those three aspects—shock, disbelief, survival mode—are the foundation of trauma. So what happens when you are being so viciously attacked?

You lose your foundation. Your view of the world crumbles. You become greatly disillusioned and come to realize a number of things:

- Safety is an illusion.
- Respect is an illusion.
- Moral values are an illusion.
- Believing this could never happen to you was an illusion.
- Believing faith in God would protect you was an illusion.

- Everything you were brought up to believe in, fear, and respect was an illusion.

Basically, your faith in humanity and society is being swept away in a matter of seconds. Aside from the physical toll of the assault, you simply feel lost. Your world has just been turned upside down. You lose faith in everything and everyone.

What do you do when you have lost your foundation? You hide. You seek shelter within yourself because there is no other place to go. Your body is trembling with the memory of what happened, and you are being terrorized by your own emotions.

The first line of defense is generally seclusion. You stay at home, you don't talk to anyone, you don't answer the phone, and you pretend that you are not home.

You try desperately to understand what has happened. You try to find one shred of logic, one single straw you can cling to. You bombard yourself with questions you don't have answers to and end up blaming yourself...because nothing else makes sense. You ask yourself:

- Could I have done anything to prevent this?
- Why did I take this way home?
- Why did I stay after all my friends left?
- What am I supposed to do?
- What should I say?
- How should I react?
- Should I hide what happened?
- Should I pretend this never happened?

- Should I say something?
- What if people talk?
- What if I went to the police?
- Would they help me?
- Would they believe me?
- What if my attacker finds me and kills me so that I cannot talk?
- What if I see him again?
- What if I am pregnant?
- What am I supposed to do?
- Who can help me?
- Who would want to be with me after this?
- Should I tell my boyfriend?
- What would he say?

Hundreds of questions, doubts, and terrifying scenarios run through your mind. You try to rationalize what happened, find someone to blame, and figure out your next move. Plans are being made and are being discarded just as fast simply because nothing makes sense anymore. You worry way too much about what other people think instead of focusing on your own well-being. Things your parents or grandparents said pop into your mind:

- Never bring shame to the family.
- Hold your head high.
- You are old enough to deal with your own problems.
- It takes two to tango.

Many trauma victims turn away from God because they blame Him for not watching out for them like they were taught He would. They can't understand how God could let this happen to them or what they did to deserve it.

The Complexity of a Traumatized Mind

I recently heard someone say, "The only way to get over trauma is by distancing yourself from it." Another person said, "I am okay with what happened. I dealt with it." And again another one said, "I have locked everything safely away in the back of my mind. I will deal with it when I am ready."

All of these statements sound logical, don't they? You try not to think about what happened, and you distance yourself from the event, and by doing so, you expect to feel better eventually. Your life should gradually go back to normal. Not quite as it used to be, but at least a new normal where you can function. You are dealing with your trauma. You push it back into the depths of your mind, and you ignore every thought or feeling that tries to come up. Eventually, you are numb toward it and toward yourself.

Then years or decades later, something happens. Someone says something, or you're in a place that stirs something within you. Before you know it, you are experiencing a major trigger. Your memories come flooding back into your consciousness. Your emotions are heightened. You feel sick to your stomach, you panic, and you feel every feeling, sensation, and emotion as if it had just happened all over again.

This is an example of what can happen if you don't release and heal your trauma. Actually, it is a very common scenario.

Other issues that a trauma survivor is subconsciously dealing with include limiting beliefs like "I am not good enough," "I am not worthy of love," "It was my own fault this happened," and "Maybe there is a reason why I deserve to suffer so much in this life." And of course, there is self-sabotaging behavior, negative self-talk, and, my all-time favorites, self-blame and self-shame. You try so hard to find the reason why this happened, and the only way to rationalize it is to believe that, in some way, it was your fault. And that is where self-blame and self-shame begin. But sadly, that's not where it ends.

Every time something does not go the way it should, you put yourself down. You treat yourself so poorly. Yes, you may even be terribly mean to yourself. If someone else did that to you, you would never talk to them again. And yet you tend to do it to yourself, blaming yourself for everything that happened and shaming yourself for everything you believe you did wrong. You can almost describe it as if there are two personas within yourself: the victim and the narcissist. Both parts are in so much pain, but rather than healing the pain, you add more to it in order to numb the pain you don't want to feel. It is a vicious cycle.

So how can you overcome it?

When you think about trauma, you automatically think about the incident, or incidents, that traumatized you. Depending on your coping mechanism, you may now experience an array of feelings, emotions, or sensations. Or you may be completely numbing yourself since the emotional toll of remembering what happened to you is just too great. So you learn to live with your trauma. You learn to shut out the painful memories and go on with your life. Yet even though you completely banish the trauma from your heart and mind, there are always those lingering and discerning thoughts. "What if my trauma comes back up?" "I don't ever want to feel this way again." "I am so afraid that I will have to face my trauma one day." "Why can't I just forget what happened and move on?"

Do you see what's happening here? You are desperately wanting to heal and have a normal, happy life, but at the same time you stop yourself from doing just that. And why? Because you are afraid. You are afraid of once again feeling what you felt when the incident happened. You are afraid of not knowing how you may feel should the trauma come back into your consciousness. You are afraid because you can't imagine who you would be without your trauma.

So how do you heal? You can not go back into the past and stop the incident from happening. You are stuck in a loop of wanting to let it go and not knowing how. That's because you focus on the incident and not on yourself.

The incident is nothing more than a part of your story, something you had to experience. What needs healing are the feelings, emotions, and sensations you held on to because of it. What needs healing is inside of you. Now this sounds pretty logical, and I am sure many of you are now wondering why I even mention it. And you are right. You know that you have to heal what is hurting within yourself. But how? And that is the million-dollar question. How can you take that incident and literally rip it out of your system like a parasite?

This is what I will explore in this book. I will discuss all of the different aspects of trauma, how trauma can alter your perception of yourself, how trauma can instill limiting beliefs and self-sabotaging behavior within you, and how to break the cycle. You have already read my story. I will use parts of my story throughout the book in order to give examples of where my limiting beliefs and self-sabotaging behaviors came from, how my parents' reaction shaped my behavior, and how I was finally able to break the cycle and find my way back to My Self.

In the next few chapters, I will talk about how trauma works within the body, what emotional triggers are and why they are actually a blessing in disguise, and how you can release your trauma once and for all. The next part will be all about trauma healing: what has to heal, how you can heal it, and which aspects are crucial to trauma healing. Then I will talk about different spiritual practices, grounding, the Chakras, and energy in general. You will get insight into many wonderful practices and exercises that can all be very helpful in your healing journey. The last part will be an introduction of unique treatment options to release trauma. Counseling is, in my opinion, an important first step after experiencing trauma. But counseling can only take you so far.

How Trauma Affects Us on All Levels

Traumatic events, no matter the type, affect not only your emotions but your whole system. A victim will be affected on a physical, mental, and emotional level, and each of these levels must be addressed individually. Let's look at sexual assault and how the thereof resulting trauma can affect a person.

The Physical Level:

Within the physical level is the memory of the physical assault. The memory of the unwanted touch. The memory of the victim's body being entered against his or her will. The memory of being helpless and powerless against the unwanted advances. When you think about the sexual act, you think about a feeling of pleasure, yet when someone is being forced into a sexual act against his or her will, it is a feeling of sheer terror and disgust. There is no pleasure whatsoever.

This feeling is unlike anything I have ever felt, and for someone who has never been sexually assaulted or raped, it's probably impossible to understand. This memory will never fade. No matter how many years pass, I will always remember how it felt when it happened.

The Emotional Level:

The emotional level holds all of the emotions you experienced when you were assaulted as well as any negative emotions that came afterward, which might come from any mental manipulation tactics your attacker used or from lack of support from your loved ones, friends, or caregivers. Yet the greatest issue on the emotional level is that the longer you have to deal with your trauma, the more intense the emotions become. What most victims don't realize is that the actual act of the assault is only a small part of the emotional toll that keeps you hostage within your own mind. How you were treated afterward, when you reached out for help, plays an even more vital role. If you were, for example, not believed, at the very least, this would instill feelings of unworthiness and abandonment.

The Mental Level:

When you are sexually assaulted, the attacker does so against your will. This means your boundaries have been crossed, and you have been greatly disrespected. This will cause the loss of self-confidence, self-esteem, and self-worth, along with feelings of insignificance and disrespect. Your mental and emotional levels are closely linked. Any emotions you feel will have an impact on your mental health. Depending on the trauma you had to experience, this can result in anxiety, depression, panic attacks, and suicidal thoughts.

As you can see, there are many levels you have to address in order to heal emotional trauma. Emotional healing is a spiritual journey, and as such, you need to treat the body as a whole in order to release any paralyzing triggers as well as self-sabotaging beliefs and behaviors, which are all aspects of PTSD.

Another Paper Cut Story

Do you remember the last time you got a paper cut? Or when you cut a slice of bread and accidentally cut into your palm? Do you remember the scab that built up over the cut? And how long it took for the scab to fall off? Have you noticed that in some areas of your body, a bleeding wound heals faster? In your mouth, for instance. A bleeding wound caused by your teeth closes up almost instantaneously. Yet a wound on your knee can have a scab for weeks.

Our bodies are self-healing. We all know that, and we tend to take it for granted. It is truly amazing, really, how broken bones grow back together, skin heals, bruises fade, and so on. But what happens when you peel off the scab before the cut underneath is healed? The wound starts to bleed again, and a new scab forms. And what happens if you use your broken leg too soon? You risk breaking it again, and then the healing will take even longer.

Healing trauma is similar. When you experience trauma, the emotional body receives a wound, a cut that is bleeding and that needs protection until it is healed. So the body does just that: It creates a protection.

This protection will be different for everyone. For me, it was weight gain. After I was raped, I began to gain weight. Everything that I went through happened when I was thin and pretty. For too long, I struggled with the belief that being thin and beautiful is dangerous, simply because it was proven to me time and time again. And since I have just recently felt ready to begin my weight loss journey, I have not had the chance to be proven otherwise.

After I began to gain weight, men left me alone. And I started to feel something resembling safety. Men stopped looking at me for more than a second and did not approach me, which suited me just fine. After I met my husband and got married three years later, I wanted to lose weight. For the first time, there was a man who loved me for who I was and not for what I looked like. I regained some of my confidence and wanted to be beautiful for him, though he already thought that I was beautiful and reminded me on numerous occasions that I should lose weight because I wanted it for myself, not because I wanted to do it for him. That right there is one of the many reasons why I love him so much.

I had lost about thirty pounds by the time I had my last dress fitting, which was two weeks before our wedding. My dress was almost too loose in the waist that day. After this fitting, I was so caught up in wedding preparations that I could not make time for the gym. On the day of our wedding, my dress almost did not fit. I had gained some of the weight back—rapidly. I was not eating any differently, but I had still gained weight.

What happened here was, in my opinion, that I tried to remove the scab from my wound before it had a chance to fully heal. My weight was my protection. And emotionally, I had not been ready to release it.

I was looking at myself in the mirror one day and suddenly realized that even though I did not like what I saw, I felt safe. And as I tried to picture myself thin, I noticed fear bubbling up. That was probably one of the biggest a-ha moments of my healing journey. I realized that I was holding myself hostage. I was afraid of letting go of the trauma. I was afraid of reliving the past. I was afraid that if I lost all of the weight and looked the way I wanted to, everything would just start all over again. I was literally terrified of being thin, or, in reality, I was terrified of men and how they would treat me if I became thin again.

Weight gain as a result of emotional trauma is such an important subject, yet it is easily overlooked. So many people are overweight as a result of emotional pain. But it is hardly recognized. Most of the time, the victims themselves don't even connect the dots.

That day when I had my epiphany, I had an appointment with my nurse practitioner, Elyse. She is a wonderful, caring woman, and I am so blessed to have her in my life. I talked to her about my realization. She looked at me thoughtfully, made a note about it on her notepad, and said, "You are so right, Sandra. I wish more people would realize that. It would help them so much in their recovery."

If you have experienced emotional trauma, you may gain weight as a form of protection in order to give yourself time to fully heal. Trying to lose that weight before the trauma is healed may cause it to come back, as the wound is still "bleeding" and needs protection. Or you may constantly sabotage your efforts without realizing it.

So, one could and should argue that a scab is the way the body heals itself physically, and weight gain can be one way the body heals itself spiritually and emotionally. That's why I would like to call this phenomenon the "spiritual yo-yo effect."

How do you know that you are ready to let go of your protection? You are ready when you realize that how you look does not reflect the person you have become on the inside. Once you reach that point, you will be ready to begin your journey toward the person you want to become. And it truly is a journey. The first step is always self-realization and self-acceptance. Understand and acknowledge that your weight is your protection and accept that this is how it had to be for you to feel safe. Never, ever punish yourself for the way you look. This will only cause another blockage within you. Resenting who you are at this very moment is closely related to being unable to practice self-love.

No matter how you feel or how you look, you are lovable! You are deserving of love. Always remember that. You need to understand that you have the power to change. But as long as you still feel safe with your weight, you are not ready. To lose the weight, work on your emotional trauma first.

For the longest time, I connected my weight loss to my wedding, an event that wasn't until later that year. Of course, I never even started to try. I basically set myself up to fail and sabotaged my efforts by emotionally eating and simply not acknowledging that I was unhappy with how I looked. But then something changed. I wanted to lose weight for me. I no longer felt that I needed my protection. I was finally able to release it. This time, my weight loss was not connected to a specific time-frame or event; it was only for my own well-being. I felt no need to emotionally eat, and I had no cravings for sweets or other treacherous foods. I practiced eating habits that I could easily get accustomed to and stick to. I even asked my husband to hold me accountable. Now that was a first! This was only possible because I worked diligently on my emotional blockages and slowly released them, and then the fear of being thin and beautiful faded away.

I would like to add that I am well aware that weight issues can stem from many different issues. I am not saying that weight gain always stems from trauma. That's just how it was in my case and how it may be for many others. When having weight issues, you should always rule out any underlying health issues, and only when everything comes back clear should you start to dig deeper. That's what I did.

Common Coping Mechanisms After Trauma

One very important thing you have to understand is that emotional trauma causes you pain, sometimes for many years. Sometimes you don't even realize that you are technically hurting, simply because you are not seeing the tell-tale signs yourself or because you try to ignore your own feelings. You might tell yourself things like:

- I am okay with what happened.
- I made peace with my past.
- I am dealing with it in my own way.
- I learned to live with it.
- I am stronger than my past.
- I locked it away safely.
- I am over it.

All of these comments sound well and good, but dealing with trauma is not healing trauma. Dealing with trauma is, quite frankly, not dealing at all. Trying to find a way to save yourself from having to confront yourself and your feelings will never work in the long run. So why do you suppress your traumatic past instead of allowing yourself to move forward and heal? Possibly, you're afraid of letting your feelings come to the surface. This is especially true if you were traumatized a long, long time ago and learned to live with the pain. You are so used to carrying this burden around with you that you probably cannot imagine what life would be without it. Humans are beings of structure and stability. Anything that could weaken your defenses is perceived as a threat, even if the threat is emotional.

Yet, if you looked closely and observed yourself, you would begin to see the tell-tale signs of suppressed negative emotions. The thing with emotional pain is that it cannot be fully suppressed. It simply shows up in a different way. A lot of the time, you chalk the signs up to bad habits. We all know what bad habits are. They are just behaviors you took on at some point and haven't been able to shake. But what if they were more? What if bad habits were actually a cry for help?

Bad habits are generally a form of emotional release. They can give you a false feeling of contentment, happiness, joy, and even fulfillment. Generally, in the beginning, when this bad habit starts to take shape, you may do it once or twice a week. But once you realize that it makes you feel good, you start to crave it. You may end up not being able to think of anything else until you give in to this bad habit and feed your hunger in order to achieve happiness.

Let's look at some possible bad habits that are directly linked to emotional pain:

Eating Disorders:

You know the happiness and sheer bliss you feel when you indulge in your favorite food. You promise yourself you'll only eat one piece of chocolate, or you'll only have a handful of chips. Yet, if you are being honest, unless you have a very strong sense of self-control, it's never just one piece, is it? When it comes to food, there is a fine line between occasional, healthy indulgence and emotional eating.

So many people are emotional eaters, yet rarely do we realize that this is a form of addiction. Partly to blame is the food industry. Just think about that commercial where a woman blissfully closes her eyes as she bites into a decadent praline, or remember how your mood changes from grumpy and whiny to strong and fearless when you take just one bite of a candy bar. Commercials are meant to sell us an emotion rather than an actual food item. Emotions sell. Every industry knows that.

Even though emotional eating is not always directly linked to trauma, there are two that, in most cases, are: binge eating and bulimia. If you suffer from this type of food addiction, you are using food as a means to reward and often punish yourself at the same time. Binge eating generally starts out as emotional eating that turns into an addiction. Yet emotional eating has been so normalized that it does not even come across as an addiction.

Bulimia is, most of the time, caused by trauma due to body-shaming or self-imposed limiting beliefs. It is also a way to punish yourself. I knew a woman who became bulimic after being gang-raped at a young age. It was her way of coping with the emotional toll. In a way, she was trying to make herself invisible. Once she moved away from her hometown, where the abuse happened, her condition improved.

The same is true for binge eating. Even though I was never prone to binge eating, I did gain quite a bit of weight after I was raped, as I discussed in the previous chapter. My reasoning was that if I weighed more, men would leave me alone, and they did. After gaining about sixty pounds, men rarely took a second glance at me. This was all well and good until I started to resent my body. On one hand, I wanted to have my old body back when I began to heal my emotional trauma, yet on the other hand I was terrified that if I were thin, everything would just happen again. It was a vicious cycle. The same is true for binge eating and bulimia.

Alcoholism and Drug Abuse:

Often, we hear about people who drank themselves into an early grave or died of an overdose. When we look into their pasts, we almost always find some form of abuse or trauma that was inadequately addressed or not addressed at all. Alcohol and hallucinogenic substances have been around for centuries. We all know that they can alter our perceptions and our behaviors. And we also know that it is, to some extent, socially acceptable behavior to partake in. In TV commercials, we see people having fun and partying on the beach while drinking rum. Or we see two sophisticated CEOs at a bar, drinking a beer. Again, we are sold an emotion: Drinking alcohol makes you happy and allows you to have fun and relax after a hard day at the office.

Let me ask you something: How often have you come home from work and just thought or declared, I had such a rough day. I need a drink! Or I need some ice cream! Even though you may not be addicted to any substance or habit, this behavior is so ingrained in you that you automatically use these measures because you believe that it will make you happy or lighten your burden. You can see this scenario in almost every movie, TV show, and magazine, and you can hear it on the radio or see it in an ad online.

So, why am I making such a huge fuss about this type of advertisement? Because we are being taught to believe that we can use tools to feel better. We are being taught that our pain, sorrow, and worries will fade away if we indulge in decadent sweets or premium alcohol. We are taught that we need something in order to feel better. So how are we supposed to know how to heal our emotional pain? Commercials don't tell us that. We are bombarded with medications that have horrendous side effects, foods and drinks that are supposed to instill a feeling of happiness within us, and so on. Yet all of these options only mask our pain.

Cutting:

Cutting is a way for a person to temporarily make the emotional pain seem less severe than the physical pain. Cutting is very often seen in teenagers. This can be a direct result of child molestation, especially if it has gone on for years and years; bullying in school; or difficult foster care. The emotional pain of the trauma is so great that it may give the victim a feeling of suffocation. Cutting temporarily gives the person a sense of relief, as if the blood that drains out of the cuts takes the emotional pain out with it. If you ask a person why he or she cuts, you will most likely hear the answer: "It just makes me feel better." Cutting is never something that just happens for the fun of it. Cutting is a subtle cry for help, even if the victim does not realize it. For the victim, it is difficult to put into words what he or she can't understand. He or she just knows that it feels wrong, painful, and disgusting.

Emotional Shopping:

When you are feeling upset, sad, angry, or just not happy, you try to find ways to make yourself happy. You try to find a rush of excitement to shift your mindset. For some, that rush is shopping. Browsing through all of the little stores in the mall, beaming in on one item that seems interesting and then picking it up, and holding it like it's the most precious thing ever. If you're one of those people who feels this way, you know it can feel as if you have just discovered the greatest treasure in the world, and you want nothing more than to take this treasure home. You are excited about your find and are on a high.

But as with any addiction, this high does not last long. Soon after you return home from your shopping spree and spread your finds out on the kitchen table to marvel at them, the high is gone and then the guilt probably sets in. The guilt over spending money you don't have. Guilt over buying something you did not need at all, and now it has no purpose other than to collect dust on a shelf somewhere in the house. And yet, if you have a shopping addiction, you just can't help yourself. The next time you go out shopping, you will find more items you just have to have. Just like with any other addiction, it can become a vicious cycle. All because you don't want to face what really needs your attention: your emotional pain.

Self-Sabotage:

One of the most common behaviors in trauma victims is self-sabotage. This behavior stems from the belief that you are not worthy of success, love, freedom, or happiness. In a way, you are punishing yourself continuously for something that was not your fault. This behavior can be a result of inadequate or nonexistent support, or it can stem from an inability to acknowledge your victimization. Maybe you cannot rationalize that what happened was out of your control. Maybe you believe that it was entirely your fault for not listening, not heeding advice, not following your intuition, or ignoring your friend's plea to be careful. And so you believe the assault is a direct result of your shortcomings.

Paradoxically, admitting that an assault was not your fault would open you up to a whole new spectrum of emotional pain. You become stuck in the tension between these two choices. You would finally have to admit to yourself that controlling your life does not equal protection. Sometimes planning your every move or planning everything to the most minuscule detail is a form of keeping a sense of control. Yet this has nothing to do with it. This is simply a way to help you ignore your pain. As long as you control every aspect of your life, your pain cannot come to the surface. Yet subconsciously, you make sure that your controlling behavior always backfires, as your subconscious mind knows that you have to deal with the emotional pain eventually.

The above examples are just a few of the most common and most obvious when it comes to suppressed emotional trauma. Not everyone will suffer in the same intensity or in the same way.

After I had been sexually abused, one of the hardest aspects for me was that I had no one to talk to. No one asked me how I was doing. No one asked me if there was anything I needed. It was just never mentioned again. I did, at some point, understand that my parents thought it would be best not to talk about it in hopes that I would eventually forget. But I never did. It always came back up. And the worst part was not the actual abuse but the lack of support.

All I really needed was someone I could talk to, open my heart to.

Being truly heard can be the first step toward emotional healing. When you see someone who portrays bad habits, the first question you should ask yourself is not, "Why does he or she do that?" Instead, ask, "What happened?"

Emotional trauma is invisible; it is silent. Way too often, do we judge people by their behavior, but we hardly ever concern ourselves with the reason behind any of it.

The Separation of Body and Soul

When you experience trauma—regardless of whether it is sexual assault, abuse, or sudden loss—something very significant is happening. Something that only you, the survivor, can rectify.

After such a violent act, many emotions, sensations, and feelings rush through you. You feel violated, sickened, and disgusted about the memory of every touch or other matter of attack. When you are being raped, not one part of it is pleasurable. When you are being violated, every fiber of your body is revolting, trying to stop it. It is burning from the inside out.

If you have ever had a Reiki treatment or another form of energy healing, you know how it feels when energy flows through your body. It tingles, it feels warm, it is relaxing, and you even may feel as if you are floating. Well, this is not at all how it feels when you are being penetrated against your will. All of your energy is rushing toward that part of your body, trying to stop the intrusion. It feels like you have just fallen on asphalt, and you pushed your hands against it to soften the impact. It's extremely tingly, to the point that it feels like your hands are on fire.

To me, it literally felt as if my own energy tried to push against my rapist's penis to stop him from penetrating me. Every fiber of my being was resenting the penetration, and I felt virtually every fiber of my being crying out in protest. I was so aware of every sensation in my body. And it was the most horrifying feeling I have ever experienced.

The days and weeks after such a violent act are the worst. You seclude yourself and try desperately to get away from the memory. You can feel everything as if it is still happening. Every touch, every thrust. You can still physically feel them, combined with the burning sensation and the disgust. You take long, extremely hot showers and try to scrub the feeling away. You feel dirty yet are incapable of washing it off. This "dirt" is not on you; it is within you.

This is when you begin to emotionally detach your mind from your body. You stop feeling like you're in your body. You separate from it. Your body is no longer a part of you because you can't stand how it feels anymore. You have lost all connection with your body. You build a protective shield that is meant to keep you from ever living through the memory again. Every time the memories come through you distance yourself even further from your body. Now it seems as if your body and your soul are two different entities. You build a wall between your body and your soul. You simply tell your body that it is left to its own devices.

Yet the body is suffering just as much as the soul and needs healing just as badly.

The body is trying to reach out to the soul over and over again, desperately trying to get its attention. Often, the body sends out signals in the form of physical pain, hives, or other ailments to get your attention. It is not uncommon for a sexual assault/rape victim to develop Fibromyalgia or other somatic disorders.

All of the emotions and sensations remain stuck within the body's cells. And at some point, these cells can't handle the heavy burden anymore. They cry out for release, and often this cry turns into physical pain, all as an effort to be heard. But at that point, you have been so disconnected from your body that you don't realize the cause of the physical pain.

Modern medicine is only beginning to understand the connection between somatic pain and the possibility of suppressed trauma. Somatic pain means physical pain. It is truly a fascinating subject. A newly emerged science, called somatic psychology, is based on the belief that emotional pain can transform into physical pain if it is not dealt with. This means that emotional trauma can present itself in physical issues if it has been suppressed for a long period of time. The amazing thing is that once the emotional trauma has been healed, the physical pain subsides.

Many people see a counselor for many years without feeling any better about their trauma. They talk about it and hash it out, but no real progress is being made. The reason is simple: Talking about the trauma does not necessarily prompt them to reconnect with their bodies and release the emotional pain and physical sensation.

So here you are. Your whole being is crying out for help. It needs healing. It needs a savior. It needs someone who will listen and take the reigns. What can you do? Quite simply put, you need to do exactly what you tried your best to avoid. You need to reconnect with your body. You need to fully embrace your whole being. This is the part where most people get stuck. Connecting with your body would mean that you would be forced to feel the same emotions and sensations that you tried so hard to suppress for so long. Yet it is the only way to heal. You need to face yourself head-on. You need to become your own warrior princess or warlord. It is a battle you need to fight against yourself. Your will to be whole again has to be stronger than your fear of feeling it all again. Once you take the first step toward healing your trauma, your cells will respond and begin releasing.

Sometimes you will feel an emotion and have a flashback, and sometimes you won't. The more you allow yourself to release, the freer, lighter, and more at one with your body you will feel.

Trauma is not something that affects solely the mind; it affects the whole being: body, mind, and spirit. And to release your traumatic past, you need to address every part of you. But where do you begin? How can you begin your journey to safely reconnect with your whole being? How can you find the courage to release all that you held on to?

Just as each trauma survivor has a different story, each healing approach will be different. There is no one-size-fits-all approach to trauma healing.

To determine which approach would be best for you, ask yourself what you feel drawn to. What do you see? Which vision makes you feel comfortable, safe, and heard? Do you see an office where you talk to someone? Do you see people practicing yoga or a similar spiritual/physical practice? Do you see yourself being in a massage parlor? Do you see yourself receiving energy healing and working with crystals?

If you allow your body and mind to work together and guide you toward the best healing approach, you will notice that your mind shifts to what would help you most. You will develop new interests and will be guided to try them out. Listen to your mind and body. They know what they need.

My trauma healing happened once I began my journey into spirituality, and so, of course, my approach to helping people release their trauma is a combination of psychological and spiritual approaches that involve the body, mind, and soul as a whole.

I help people release their trauma through energy work (Reiki), somatic psychology approaches (trauma coaching and mentoring), meta-psychology approaches (Traumatic Incident Reduction), mindfulness (guided meditation, visualizations, and journaling), and ancestral healing through the Akashic Records. Combining these approaches into one holistic trauma healing program will bring fast and lasting results.

Trauma is something that you had to experience, but it is not something you have to live with for the rest of your life. You have every right to kick it to the curb, stand up, brush off your clothes, and live a happy and successful life.

Angelica's Story

When Angelica (name changed out of respect for privacy) reached out to me, she was searching for answers. She was looking for someone who could help her determine whether she had healed her trauma fully, as she thought, or whether something was still there.

During her Free Consultation with me, she mentioned that she wished she could just cut off her breasts. She said that she had been molested when she was a teenager and, ever since then, had felt disgusted by this body part. She further mentioned that she had not cried in over a decade.

After talking to her and hearing about the above-mentioned issues, as well as the question of whether she had healed her trauma or not, I knew that she had, in fact, not healed. She had merely been suppressing her trauma for a very long time.

Remember my last chapter, where I talked about the separation of body and soul? Wanting to remove body parts because you can't stand the ever-present memory of the unwanted touch is a classic example of not wanting to feel a certain sensation and therefore distancing yourself from the body. But cutting off body parts won't solve that problem. Only healing the associated trauma will. And that is what Angelica was about to do.

Angelica lived with her father from when she was four years old. Her mother had divorced him and after remarrying, moved to another country, not being able to take her daughter with her.

Her father always described her as his gem, his angel, the perfect child. He praised her and told anyone who wanted to hear how much he loved and adored her. But behind closed doors, the world of a young, innocent child looked very different.

Angelica loved school; it was her escape. She was an A student and could not wait to graduate and leave her home for good so she could escape her father's abuse. You see, she was beaten by her father on a regular basis—not enough to leave visible marks, of course, because that would raise questions about the validity of his claims of being a doting father.

He also started showing a sexual interest in her when she was six years old. At first, he stole a kiss here and there and touched her inappropriately on several occasions. But as she got older, he became more demanding. One day, Angelica confided in her older brother about their father's advances on her. Her brother was shocked and confronted their father. What happened next was the worst beating Angelica ever received at her father's hand. What she learned that day was that asking for help would only make it worse.

Angelica fought him off and denied him her body any way she could. During one of our sessions, she told me that she'd have rather endured her father's beatings than his inappropriate advances. But then, she said, her father used a different tactic to get what he wanted. He threatened to not allow her to attend school unless she gave in to him. This tortured Angelica more than any beating she ever received at his hand. School was her escape, her sanctuary. On so many occasions, her father forced her to stay home. But she never gave in, until one day when she was fourteen.

After she had been forced to stay home for weeks, she could not take it anymore and agreed to go to her father's bedroom just so she could go back to school. She decided that she would just tune out, like she always did whenever her father beat her. She told herself that she could just escape into her own mind, let him do whatever it was he wanted to do, and never look back. Even though she did the best she could to forget what happened that night, the memories haunted her until she was finally ready to face and release them.

This incident was the reason Angelica wanted to cut off her breasts. She could not shake the memory of her father's touch. But even more so, she was disgusted by her body, disgusted by her father, and so alone. She told me during our session that she threw away the dress she had worn that night so that she would never have to see it again and be reminded of what she had agreed to do in desperation.

After this incident, her father never touched her again inappropriately or forced her to stay home to get his way. She finished school and left the country to start a new life as far away from her father as she could.

When Angelica and I started her healing journey with Traumatic Incident Reduction Sessions, she was very open about the facts but closed off about her emotions. That came as no surprise to me since she had told me that she hadn't cried in over a decade. She also told me that she had no good memories from her childhood despite the fact that all of her other relatives were wonderful, caring people whom she loved very much.

"I watched an influencer's You Tube video once, and he said that childhood should be the most joyful time in our lives, but my childhood was never joyful. I can't recall one single moment that was ever joyful," Angelica said.

In our third session, she cried. She was surprised that she did, but I reassured her that this was a very good thing because she was finally allowing her emotions to come out. During our fourth session, she told me that after she had went home from work a few days earlier, she had cried for hours on end. And afterward, she had felt so much better.

Crying is so healing, especially when we have suppressed our feelings for so long. Opening up emotionally can be like a breaking dam. At first, the walls explode and water spews out, destroying everything in its path, but once most of the water has been drained from that man-made lake, the water-power ceases, and the flow of the water becomes calmer and gentler. It is the same with bottled-up emotions.

Since that evening, Angelica had also begun to laugh at funny TV shows, which was something she had not done in years. In essence, she had allowed herself to truly feel again. That was a huge step forward. But we still had one more task at hand: releasing the trauma her father had caused.

In our sixth session, she did the final part of the Traumatic Incident Reduction Session Sequence: releasing the incident. Without hesitation, Angelica talked through the most traumatic event with her father: the night she had gone willingly into his bedroom. She released the incident with ease and, immediately after, reported that the sickening feeling and the physical memory of her father's touch were gone. She no longer felt the need to cut off her breasts. She had released that trauma from her body, mind, and spirit.

In our next session, she told me about a nice memory she had with her uncle. It was so wonderful to see that now that the trauma had been released—it was no longer suppressed, and there was no longer a need to suppress anything—the happy memories she had suppressed because of the trauma were coming back to the surface.

She began to remember the good times of her childhood because the dark times did not overshadow them anymore.

This is an important aspect of trauma and trauma healing. When we force ourselves to suppress traumatic memories, emotions, and sensations, we also suppress the good ones. And with that, we don't allow ourselves to feel, because we can't fully embrace and feel the good without freeing the bad.

Once you have released your trauma, you no longer have to be afraid that it might come back up again—because it is just gone. And then you are free to feel everything. The love, the joy, the sheer freedom, and happiness.

We always say to our children, "When you find the right one, you will know." And that is so true. I knew when I met my husband that he was the one. And it is the same with releasing trauma. Once you have released your trauma, you will know for sure that it is gone. There is no doubt about it.

Angelica released the trauma with her father during only one session sequence of six sessions. That's all it took. She actually just sent me a text message saying, "Life is so good!"

Feeling Whole Again

The disconnection of body and soul is more profound than you may think. So, in this chapter, I want to go deeper into this subject. I have already talked about how the disconnect can happen, and shared Angelica's story. However, it may not just be resulting from sexual assault; it can happen from any type of trauma. Anything that robs you of your peace of mind, feeling of safety, and control can cause a separation of your body and your soul.

How do you know that you are living with this disconnect? Here are a few examples of how you may feel:

1. You feel lost.
2. You feel so very alone.
3. You feel anxious in big crowds.
4. You feel as if a part of you is missing.
5. You feel as if you don't belong.
6. You feel out of place.
7. You are unable to meditate.
8. You are unable to find peace in stillness.
9. Silence drives you crazy.
10. Silence terrifies you.
11. Being alone terrifies you.

Here is how you would feel if your body and soul were one:

1. You feel at peace.
2. You feel whole.
3. You feel content with who you are.
4. You feel safe.
5. You feel as if you are exactly where you are supposed to be.
6. You welcome stillness.
7. You don't mind being alone. Instead, you find comfort and healing in solitude.

Reconnecting body and soul generally happens gradually, on its own, the more you heal from trauma. However, some people may struggle with it even though the trauma they had to experience does not haunt them anymore.

Reconnecting body and soul is a journey to the center of your being. For some, it is the most terrifying journey they have ever made. Some people would rather free climb Mount Everest than descend into the depth of themselves.

Fear is always what holds people back. I talked about this before. You fear what you don't understand; you fear the unknown. You don't know what you will find within yourself, and that might scare you. If you fear reconnecting with yourself, it might mean that you're afraid you will never come back from it. Remember what I said in an earlier chapter? You are the one you can never get away from. And so it is understandable if you are afraid to open aspects of yourself that you believe you don't want to know about.

However, if you think about this rationally, this does not make any sense, because how can you be afraid of yourself? This is you that you are talking about. There is no hidden dark secret within yourself. There is no alter ego. There is no Dr. Jekyll and Mr. Hyde. You will not turn into the Hulk the moment you descend into the depth of your being.

On the contrary, people who are disconnected from themselves have a greater chance of mental, emotional, or personality issues than those who are fully connected and at peace with who they are.

The process of soul reconnection is accompanied, for many, by a "dark night of the soul." I am sure you have heard of that term before. So, let's talk about it for a moment. The dark night of the soul, in essence, means that you are allowing yourself to experience yourself through your shadow self. The shadow self is the part of you that holds all of the negativity, everything you don't want to see, and everything you don't want to become.

In order to heal, you have to work with your fear, not against it. Fear is an illusion. Fear is a creation of your mind to protect yourself from the unknown. But in order to release and grow, you have to lean into your fear. And by leaning into your fear, you can release it. Once you understand what you are afraid of, you can work with that new-found knowledge and transform your fear.

And the more you lean into your fear, giving it love, compassion, and the freedom to convey its message, the easier it will become to release it and, with that, reconnect your body and your soul.

Don't be afraid of your own emotions. Allow them to come forward and be released. And if you feel overwhelmed by it, please reach out.

Bridget's Story

In the chapter "The Separation of Body and Soul," I briefly touched on chronic, or rather somatic, pain and the link to trauma. In this chapter, I will be sharing the incredible story of my client Bridget, who released her chronic pain by releasing her traumatic past. I am so grateful that she allowed me to share her story, because it is simply awe-inspiring!

Bridget had suffered from chronic lower back pain ever since she suffered a back injury in her early twenties. She had been diagnosed with Multiple Sclerosis in her mid-thirties. From working in a factory for many years, the degenerative disk disease in her lower back had worsened, and the pain had become almost unbearable, to the point where she had to quit her job. When she went to seek help for her pain once again, the doctor at the clinic explained to her that the perception of pain was created in the brain. At that time, Bridget did not understand the meaning of what the doctor had said. Today, Bridget understands that the doctor's diagnosis was correct, but she also knows that it lacked the insight she would have needed in order to connect the dots. And so, at the time, she dismissed the doctor's diagnosis and decided that he was simply wrong and insensitive.

When Bridget and I met, she was ready to release her trauma but had no idea how much her life would change after only a handful of sessions. She had been referred to me by a mutual friend, and we began our sessions in November of 2019. She had been through a lot in her life, including molestation and abuse from her father, an overall abusive family, two narcissistic relationships, alcohol and drug abuse, and much more.

When we met, she was in a very dark place, but she knew that she wanted and needed to release her trauma in order to get her life back on track. So, we began her healing journey with traumatic incident reduction sessions, or short T.I.R.

In T.I.R. we work on one issue until it is resolved, and then we move on to the next. This usually takes about five sessions depending on the issues involved.

After discussing everything that was going on in her life and compiling a list of possible issues to work on, Bridget chose to begin her journey by discussing her father. He had been abusive and narcissistic, and he had molested her on several occasions when she was a child. The incident she chose to work on was a movie night that had been branded into her consciousness.

Her parents were divorced. Bridget spent most of her time with her mother and visited her father on a mostly bi-weekly basis.

Bridget's father used to scratch her back whenever they sat on the couch watching TV, which a young, innocent Bridget greatly enjoyed. (And why wouldn't she? I remember back-rubs that I received from my grandmother, and those are fond memories.) But then, when she was eleven years old, his behavior changed. Instead of only rubbing her back, his hands wandered to her shoulders and to the front, where he started caressing her breasts.

This behavior confused young Bridget. She did not understand what was happening but knew that it was wrong. I can so relate to that. Remember my story? The same happened to me by the hand of that stable master when I was twelve. Only, in my case, it was a stranger. In Bridget's case, it was her own father, which adds a whole new level of inappropriateness.

On one particular day, Bridget's father had rented a movie for himself and his twelve-year-old daughter to watch. The title was Hamburger: The Motion Picture, which is classified as "sex comedy" and was clearly not the right type of movie for a twelve-year-old girl. As they began watching the movie, her father had his feet up on the couch, and he motioned for her to come rest between his legs while leaning against him.

The movie and the sexual scenes, which she could not make any sense of, made her feel extremely uncomfortable, and she tried to understand why her father was making her watch it. And then she noticed that something hard was poking into her lower back. Bridget thought it was the remote control and tried to move it because it was hurting her. Little did she know that this was her father's erect penis. As she innocently tried to grab it in order to remove what she thought was the remote control, her father jolted and took her hand away. He made her continue leaning back against him even though it physically hurt her. Bridget did not know what she was leaning against, but she felt a growing unease, especially after her father's reaction, so she sat up and moved to the other end of the couch. She sat there, quiet and confused, until it was time for her to go back home to her mom.

During the course of our sessions, Bridget came to the profound realization that the lower back pain she suffered from was psychological pain from that very incident. The realization hit her after she had released the trauma and could look at it from a detached perspective. Her back hurt in the exact same spot where her father's erection had pressed against her. And that profound realization released that pain.

When you have a profound realization, it is like a jolt that goes through your body, as if a huge bell just rang and you feel its vibration running through you. When you have a profound realization, you just know that it is the truth. And this truth can turn into an incredible mindset shift.

Bridget still suffers from degenerative disk syndrome—that has not changed—but the pain now only occurs when she overdoes it with straining work, and then it subsides very quickly, which it never used to do. The constant pain she was in for so many years is gone. And she now understands what the doctor had told her all those years ago. The excruciating physical pain she felt in her lower back was somatic pain from that one terrible experience.

Bridget had just released decades-old trauma and would never be haunted by it again. From that moment on, her relationship with her father changed. She would no longer allow him to be verbally abusive and set strict boundaries. She regained her self-confidence and self-respect. Her father no longer had power over her. All of this happened through the course of only five T.I.R. sessions.

But this was just one part of her amazing transformation. In her mid-thirties, Bridget developed MS. She was on medication and still battled the pain on a daily basis, and she also suffered from side effects from her many medications, which were combined with drug and alcohol abuse.

After releasing the trauma her father had caused, we moved our focus to her ex-boyfriend. He was a very violent, controlling, manipulative, and dangerous man. He was your classic narcissist. Bridget had to live through manipulation, aggression, physical and emotional abuse, and even death threats.

Bridget spent many years with this man, and there were many traumatic events for us to look at and work through. After having completed a full T.I.R. session sequence, she understood the work and value in it and chose the one subject that had traumatized her the most in her time with her ex-boyfriend. In this particular scenario, her ex-boyfriend had forced her into an abortion and demanded that she also get her tubes tied, which she did. On the day of the procedure, he tried to guilt-trip her into killing his child. He behaved extremely erratically and violently, and he was verbally abusive. She was afraid for her life, totally confused and just terrified by the whole situation. She was torn between wanting this child and not wanting it, as she kept replaying the moment in her head when her ex-boyfriend had threatened to kill both her and the baby should she carry out her pregnancy. This traumatic incident was not only governed by fear for her life, but it was also governed by guilt, shame, and so many what ifs.

We began working on this issue in February 2020 but had to interrupt our sessions because she was one of the unlucky ones who contracted Covid. She fought with this virus for a good six to eight weeks. It just would not leave her be. During this time, her doctor asked her to stop taking her MS medication because it seemed to interfere with her recovery. She was understandably very afraid to stop her medication because she expected to be in a lot of pain.

And then the miracle happened. As she was recovering and becoming more active again, she realized that gardening did not leave her in as much pain as it used to. And the soreness she felt left rather quickly compared to what she had been used to for such a long time. At that time, we had just finished our sessions on the incident with her ex-boyfriend, and she then felt that it was just a story. She had no emotional connection to it anymore.

When you think about MS and the situation she was in, you can draw a clear line. She was constantly tensed up out of fear of what her ex-boyfriend would do next. Not strong or brave enough to leave him and yet prepared for anything. She was abused physically, mentally, and emotionally while still being traumatized by what her father did to her. After she released both issues, her body could relax, and she was not feeling the need to tense up anymore. And with that, her body and her nervous system released and healed the physical trauma that was a direct result of the emotional trauma she had to experience.

Bridget's journey is truly inspiring. She had the courage to face her trauma head-on and then released it. What she gained was more freedom than she could ever have imagined. Not only did she transform emotionally, but she also did not need drugs or alcohol to help her function any longer, and on top of everything, she released her physical pain. And do you know how many sessions that took? TEN. It took ten weekly sessions in total to release decades of trauma.

Bridget has always been drawn to music. As a teenager, she taught herself to play the guitar and has been writing songs and composing music ever since. In her early twenties, she had been invited to a recording studio to record her first album, which could have been the beginning of a wonderful career. But her father sabotaged her shot at success by refusing to lend her the money she would have needed for the trip. He belittled Bridget and made her believe that she would never make it as a singer.

She mentioned this incident during the course of our sessions, and we worked on it through coaching. The next week, she told me that she had started putting her songs out on various online platforms. She stepped out of her comfort zone and did something that terrified her. I was so proud of her that day!

Today, Bridget is no longer afraid to call herself a singer and songwriter. Her songs have always been her outlet for her emotions. For years, she has sung about her trauma. It was a way for her to cope. Now that she has begun her transformation, I am looking forward to seeing how her music will reflect that.

Check her out and follow her transformation with me at @bridgetmusic on YouTube, or

@bridgetmusicofficial on TikTok, and Facebook.

Emotional Triggers

The other day, I experienced a very intense trigger brought on by an online game my husband and I started to play. In case you were wondering, the game in question is World of Warcraft Classic. That evening began rather pleasantly. We set up the game, chose our characters, waited in the queue, and, when it was our turn, started our journey from level one to level sixty. All well and good. At first, we were playing solo, and then my husband started playing with some friends. I continued on solo, as I was in a different area. I had a lot of fun and was about three levels ahead of my husband. Next thing I knew, my husband had caught up to me at record speed. That's when the trigger hit me out of the blue. I suddenly felt worthless, like a failure, as if no matter what I tried, I always failed. Whoa! Where did that come from? I went from enjoyable game play to bawling my eyes out in a matter of seconds.

The funny thing is that this is not a game of competition. There are no winners or losers. So, feeling the way I did, especially to such an extreme, made no sense at all. I was not jealous of my husband for being better than me. He had decades of experience in computer games that I did not have, so it was no wonder that he was better. Yet I felt so low and worthless, like a complete failure.

That night, I woke up around 4:00 a.m., feeling so sad and hurting so much. My heart was aching. I got up, as sleep was not an option anymore, and as soon as I sat down on the couch, I started to cry. Tears just kept on pouring out of me for a good hour.

I knew that what I was experiencing was a major emotional release. I also knew that what had happened the day before was a trigger. Neither my husband nor that game was the problem. It was just a trigger. So, I began to look within myself to try and find the actual root cause of the issue. When had I felt this low and insignificant before? I remembered a couple of incidences in my childhood and teenage years when I had felt that way. It was nothing major—nothing that would classify as trauma in any way—but it had made me feel pretty worthless.

The more I brought those incidences back into my conscious mind, the more came up. And at the same time, the easier it became for me to understand what had happened. I had felt that I was not good enough, that no matter how hard I tried, I would always fail. I used to feel like that every now and then as a child and teenager. And I guess right then was the time for these emotions to come to the surface and be released.

I felt so bad for my husband, as he did not know how to make sense of my emotional outbursts or how to help me. Once I explained to him what had happened and talked a bit about the memories that came up, he began to understand. He understood that this was something I had to go through by myself. And for the next couple of days, we played side by side and had lots of fun, and there were no more tears.

Triggers can be very scary and nerve-racking. We try to understand why we suddenly feel the way we feel but are too afraid to lean into the triggers and learn from them. But an emotional trigger is not the enemy; rather, it is a guiding light toward what requires attention and healing within ourselves. I am honestly so glad that this trigger came up, as it allowed me to release some of my self-sabotaging behavior patterns. Feeling not worthy or not good enough was holding me back from truly embracing my dreams and my purpose, until now!

So, let's recap. What is a trigger? A trigger is an emotional response brought on by a memory of a situation that happened a long time ago and that was never healed. It could be a traumatic event or a violation of a core value. Triggers happen when you are confronted with a situation that brings on a physical, mental, or emotional response to something you experienced before. When you are being severely triggered, you may even experience symptoms of PTSD.

Does that make a trigger a bad thing? Not in the least. Even though triggers can get emotionally exhausting, they are a good thing because they show you what needs healing within yourself. They are a road map to your own health and well-being.

How can you release those triggers and heal your trauma? You must embrace those negative and disruptive emotions, sensations, and feelings, then figure out what they want to tell you. You must dig deep and unearth the root of your anger and resentment.

The most important thing is to not resent those triggers; embrace them, love them, and acknowledge them. After all, they show you the part of yourself that needs your attention. To be whole, you must embrace your dark side and bring it to the light so it can be released.

On the lines below, I encourage you to write down situations where you were triggered. Take a step back and observe. Think back to that moment and analyze your behavior and your feelings. Why were you triggered? What was the underlying emotion?

Understanding your triggers is a huge step toward releasing them and, along with that, the trauma that caused them.

Perfectionism,
Control, and OCD

What is the one aspect that perfectionism, control, and OCD have in common? They all stem from trauma. Trust me. Ask someone if she is a perfectionist or a control freak, and when that person says yes, ask if she had any trauma in her life. I guarantee you that nine times out of ten, the answer is yes.

As I am working on this chapter, we are in the middle of the Covid-19 pandemic. When this whole pandemic started to escalate and we had to homeschool and practice social distancing and extreme caution while running errands, my thoughts went to all of the already-traumatized souls who had to completely adjust their routines. And my heart went out to those souls who would be traumatized by this horrific event.

Even if you haven't lost a loved one, if you are not a frontline worker, and you have been able to avoid catching the virus, no one is getting out of this event unscathed.

During this pandemic, I spent some time re-watching some of my favorite TV shows. At this time, it was Criminal Minds. Fifteen seasons of unraveling the minds of serial killers. As horrific as most cases are, this show fascinates me. The mind and the resulting behavior are like a puzzle. There is a reason why we behave the way we do. Almost every serial killer that the BAU analyzes on the show has been through major trauma in the past, and the need to be violent was a direct link to that trauma.

But let's not talk about the minds of serial killers. I'll leave that to the experts on the subject. I only mentioned this particular show because it had such a huge impact on my work as a trauma coach. There is always a reason for your behavior. To change the behavior, you have to connect the dots. You have to find the root cause, understand it and its effect on you, and release the associated emotions. And that's what I essentially do during my sessions.

So let's dive into the mind and the mysteries of perfectionism, control, and OCD. I can tell you that whenever I discuss this subject with my clients, I can see a huge shift happening within them. Something just clicks, and those behaviors just make sense. And then the most beautiful and inspiring thing happens: My clients become aware of when they are portraying these behaviors, and then they stop themselves in their tracks, acknowledge their need for control, and consciously try to release this need.

Here is what's important to remember: When you were being traumatized, no matter the story, it was out of your control. Having control taken from you leaves you powerless. What can you do when you don't have any control? What can you do when you are at the mercy of the person who traumatized you? Frankly, not much.

When you are over the initial shock and begin to pick up the pieces that were your life, you still feel powerless. Once you had control taken away from you in a violent way—regardless of whether it was rape, a car accident, or the loss of a loved one—your perception changed. Now, the sense of being in control is still gone, and yet you don't realize that. There is an empty space in your body, mind, and spirit where the sense of control was. And slowly but surely, you try to fill that void. But the issue is that you can't fill a void you don't know exists. So you try to compensate. Gradually, you start to mimic control by trying to control everything within your reach. But the thing is, you never feel in control or satisfied with yourself and your accomplishments, and so you try harder and harder.

This need for control can become obsessive if the trauma is not being addressed. It may begin with little things, like the house needing to be in perfect order. Nothing can be in the wrong place. You may get agitated when the chair at the dinner table is not in the exact right spot. It may get so bad that you are compelled to do things in threes (just an example). All because it makes you feel as if you are in control.

But the thing is, you are not in control; your trauma is.

The same is true for perfectionism. You try to be perfect, behave perfectly, or keep your surroundings perfect. There are different reasons for this depending on the type of traumatic incident you had to experience. You may try and make yourself perfect by having perfect clothing and wearing makeup so that people don't see what lies underneath the surface. You may try to keep your house impeccable because the cleanliness of your house is something you can control, and if it is messy, it would reflect on the mess you feel is inside you, below the surface. Keeping your surroundings impeccable is within your control. It makes sense that everything has its proper spot. And yet you never feel satisfied. There is always that nagging feeling of emptiness within you. Something is always missing, but rather than focusing on what is missing, you suppress that feeling because it scares you, and you focus even more on perfectionism and control.

Tell me this: When you think about giving up some of your control—let's say giving your husband responsibility over the laundry—how does that make you feel? Are you totally fine with it, or are your palms sweating? Is your heart racing? Do you have the unignorable need to tell him how to fold the towels correctly?

How about the dishwasher? Is he filling it, and if so, are you rearranging the dishes when he is done? What about leaving that chair an inch to the side of its original place? Does that make you crazy just thinking about it? These were just a couple of general examples. Even though these examples may not resonate with you, I am sure you understand what I am getting at.

Depending on the depth of the emotional wound, perfectionism and control can become excessive. They can become a desperate notion to regain some form of normality. It can go so far that you try to control every move of a loved one or family member. You can even become abusive in your need to stay in control.

As a victim of this type of abusive treatment, you have to realize that at its root is pain. This is something I had to consciously embrace not too long ago. It can be tough to be compassionate and forgiving when you are being bullied, manipulated, threatened, and abused by people who were supposed to treat you as one of their own. But understanding that the root issue has nothing to with you is the only way you can rise above it.

If trauma has not been addressed for many years, perfectionism can become a nuisance. At some point, you will crack under the immense pressure of being perfect or making everything perfect all the time. Then you will begin to shame yourself for your perfectionism. This causes extra trauma, limiting beliefs, and self-sabotaging behavior. It can become a downward spiral.

Perfectionism is a silent cry for help. By healing your trauma, you can slowly release the need to control every aspect of your life. By healing your trauma, you can find your way back to yourself.

Healing trauma means rediscovering yourself. It means loving the person you used to be and embracing the person you have become. The beauty is that once you begin to heal your emotional pain, the need for control and perfectionism, as well as OCD, will gradually fade away.

Now I encourage you to observe yourself and see if there are parts of your life you practice strict control and perfectionism in. Ask yourself if you show mild to moderate signs of OCD. And then try to find the root cause. Follow that feeling that urges you to do the things you do. Where did that feeling come from? What happened at that ground-zero moment? After you find it, look at it, observe it, and understand it. This would be an excellent time to make use of the journaling technique I mentioned at the beginning of this book.

Laurie's Story

In the last chapter, I talked about perfectionism, control, and OCD. In this chapter, I am sharing a profound and life-changing a-ha moment my client Laurie had in our very first session.

Laurie came to me because she was looking for a way to release the unbearable pain she still carried from her mother's unnecessary death. Her mother had been brutally murdered. The violent crime shook Laurie to her core. She could not make sense of it. There was no sense to be made. To this day, no one really knows what happened. No proof has been discovered, and no one was ever charged with this senseless crime, even though everyone close to Laurie's mother was certain that it was her abusive ex-partner.

This horrible incident happened when Laurie was in her late twenties, almost two decades ago. When we met, she was seeking help to finally be able to release her trauma for her children's sake. She did not want to burden her daughters with the emotional toll of her trauma. She wanted to raise her girls to become strong, empowered women, and she knew she could only do that if she came from a place of empowerment herself.

During our first session, she asked me why she felt this urge to always have everything under control. She had to make sure that the chairs in the dining room were always in the right spot, that everything was cleaned up right after being used, and so on and so forth. The mere thought of something being out of place drove her up the wall.

I explained to Laurie that control, and the resulting OCD, was a coping mechanism. What had happened to her mother made no sense at all. And so she desperately tried to bring sense back into her life. Having the chair in exactly that spot just made sense.

Once I explained that to her, I could see a shift going through her. She looked at me with big eyes and said, "You know, that makes so much sense!" And after a brief moment of contemplation, she said, "I have had years of therapy, and no one was ever able to explain that to me."

When we met for our next session, she told me that what I had explained to her really made her think, and the more she internalized it, the more she understood the impact it had. That weekend, when her kids were playing out in the yard, she purposefully did not go out right away to clean up the toys. She wanted to observe how she reacted. And when she felt the need to clean it up, she told herself that it was okay, that nothing bad would happen if the toys stayed out there on the lawn for a little while longer.

She smiled when she told me that her husband had asked if she was feeling all right, as he had never seen his wife not caring about stuff lying around.

Laurie was able to release the emotional pain from her mother's death with ease. And it all started with a little insight into why she needed control so obsessively. That little bit of information caused a quantum leap forward in her healing journey.

"You can't move into the future
with a mindset of the past."

–Sandra Cooze

How to Release Trauma

In theory, the concept of releasing trauma is quite simple. But applying this concept can become quite the challenge. I say challenge because each and every one of us can heal from our trauma. We simply have to decide that we will do just that.

To heal from trauma, you first must understand that what happened is part of your story and will always remain a part of your story. Then you must decide that this part of your story is over. You have to get up, brush off your clothes, and turn your back on this part of your story. Your past can only continue to hurt you if you give it the power to do so.

And then you put the pieces of your life back together. One piece at a time, like a puzzle. You have to relearn to love yourself despite your scars. You have to learn to respect yourself for what you have overcome. You have to challenge yourself to always be stronger and more determined than the person you were yesterday.

Despite everything, you are still here. You must replace your fears, doubts, and worries with love, courage, and determination. Your past is not what defines you, but whether you choose to fight for yourself to overcome it is.

The most important part of trauma healing is to never give up and to never give in. There are many wonderful trauma healing approaches out there. Counseling is just one of them. Think outside the box. Believe me, the answer is out there. The right person with the right modality for you is out there. If one approach does not work, try another one. If one counselor or psychologist can't help you get the results you are hoping to have from your time together, look for another one.

Never give up! Find the right approach for your emotional healing. You shouldn't have to suffer for the rest of your life because of something that was not even your fault. You should never have to feel like taking your own life because of unbearable pain. You should never have to feel like no one can help you. Trauma can be healed. All you need to do is find the right approach for you. Period!

What is Trauma Healing Really About?

Healing trauma is not about the incident; it's about releasing the limiting beliefs, self-sabotaging behavior, and emotional blockages that were created because of the incident.

The incident, in itself, is just a part of your story. It is something that happened to you. But it is nothing that should control you. So, in order to heal your trauma, you have to realize that you are in control, not the trauma. That is the fundamental difference between being a trauma victim and being a trauma survivor. Trauma victims are controlled by their traumatic pasts, and trauma survivors have decided that their trauma will no longer be in control.

However, entering the stage of trauma survivor does not mean you have healed. It simply means that you are one step closer to truly healing and releasing your past. As a trauma survivor, if you are still being triggered, you are still a captive of your past. Once you are truly healed from your trauma, there are no triggers or uncomfortable emotions left.

I can still recall every incident of my trauma in detail, but I have no emotions attached to it. I am so detached from my story that I often feel as if I am telling someone else's. There is simply no trauma left.

To heal your trauma, you have to self-reflect. You have to go deep within yourself and observe. Whenever you are being triggered or are feeling less than at least neutral, you have to look for the cause within yourself. There, you will find the answer.

To heal your trauma, you have to love that very part of yourself that you tried to lock away for so long. The part of you that is hurting is the part of you that you have to nurture in order to heal.

A little further along in this book, I will talk about the Chakras, grounding, energy balance, and even a salt bath, among other things. Each of these chapters has information that can help you on your journey. Give them the benefit of the doubt, test them out, play with them, and see if my suggestions help you. There is no cookie-cutter approach to trauma healing, so some of my suggestions may resonate with you, and some may not. That is perfectly fine! Pick the ones that intrigue you and start there.

Mind Over Ego

The ego is an interesting aspect of yourself. When you don't understand its function, it controls you. But once you do understand it, you can take back control and thrive. So, what is the ego, and why is it so controlling?

The ego is that little voice in your head that stops you from stepping out of your comfort zone and challenge yourself. It is the creator of negative self-talk and limiting beliefs.

To fully understand the purpose of the ego, we have to go back in time, way back to our ancestors, the Neanderthals. The Neanderthals were hunters and gatherers who lived in caves. Their lives were not easy. The animals they hunted for in order to get food were, for the most part, much larger and fiercer than any animal we know of today. During those days, the ego was a hunter's best friend. It warned them of danger.

Do you know the feeling you get when you sense someone behind you? Skin prickles. Goose bumps. And those tiny hairs on the back of your neck that stand up straight. That is your ego sending signals to your brain, and your brain sends signals to the little hairs on your neck to warn you.

So, in essence, the ego is your very own built-in warning system. That's a good thing, right? Well, yes and no. You see, no warning system is foolproof. Any warning system can malfunction. That is not to say that you have a malfunctioning warning system. Not at all. You just have to recalibrate it and adjust it to modern times. You don't have to be warned because a large mammoth is coming up behind you, right? But your ego behaves as if you do. Because even though we did evolve as a species, our egos did not.

Your ego is a master at talking you down and keeping you stuck where you are. Your ego is "afraid" of allowing you to try new things, step out of your comfort zone, or even do something differently. When it comes to trauma, this can be the major cause of you not being able to release. You are simply afraid of letting go, of having to go through it again, and of not knowing who you would be without the pain. And of course, you also have the fear of what other people might think if you truly release your trauma and heal from something so horrible that you should never be able to heal from it.

How can you recalibrate your ego? The answer is quite simple: You must challenge yourself. You must prove to yourself that you are stronger than your fear. You have to step out of your comfort zone and witness that you can do what you set your mind to.

Depending on your mental and emotional state, adjusting your ego can be quite triggering. That is okay. Triggers are not the enemy, as I have mentioned in an earlier chapter. Triggers are a guiding light toward what needs healing. And if you can adjust your mindset to see them as just that, you can take a step back from your trauma and observe it. Baby steps are key to adjusting your mindset and releasing your triggers.

Remember that whatever you had to experience has already happened. It is in the past, but the mind and the body can keep you in the presence of it for decades. So, with that in mind, think about something that makes you feel uncomfortable, worried, and uneasy. For example, changing up your routine a bit. Let's say you have the morning routine of getting out of bed, going to the bathroom, and then preparing your coffee or tea and your lunch for work. Then you take a shower and get ready to leave the house. This is your daily routine, your anchor. It works. It is a good routine for you. But what if you changed it up a bit? What if you took your shower first and then made your coffee or tea? What if you chose to eat at the cafeteria instead of at your desk? Eating at the cafeteria might terrify you because you feel threatened in big crowds. So, challenge yourself. Ask yourself: "What is the worst that can happen?" The room is full of people, men and women alike. Everyone is there for the same reason: to eat and chat with friends and coworkers.

Let's say you have been going to the cafeteria for the past few days and have always found a spot away from everyone else. You always ate alone and just watched people. You began to feel comfortable because nothing ever happened. You started to feel safe going to the cafeteria. So, then you could challenge yourself once more. Maybe you noticed another woman sitting all by herself, looking scared or worried. And maybe you got the feeling that she might be in a similar situation as you were just a little while ago. So, one day, you may challenge yourself by going over to her with your tray and asking if you can share her table. And then you both go from there.

What is happening here is that you are gradually stepping out of your comfort zone. And with that, you are gradually and naturally releasing triggers. Your ego is also gradually adjusting to the new boundaries you set.

This was just a basic example of how you can gradually heal by challenging yourself. So, what are your ideas for challenging yourself? Write some ideas in the lines below. If you have a friend you trust deeply, ask him or her to hold you accountable so you can stretch your limits. Allow that person to be a part of your healing journey. This can be a wonderful experience for both of you. It will help you learn to trust and open up to someone else, and your friend may feel empowered because he or she can support you on your journey and make a difference in your life.

How could you step out of your comfort zone? List some ideas:

How to Stop Negative Self-Talk

In the last chapter, I talked about the ego and how it can stop you from stepping out of your comfort zone. In this chapter, I want to talk about its role in your self-imposed limiting beliefs and self-sabotaging behavior.

But first, let's get one thing right out into the open: The ego can a nasty b*tch.

The ego is that friend you don't want in your life but keep out of obligation. The ego is that friend who gets off on putting you down. It is your ego that causes the negative self-talk. It repeats your negative beliefs of yourself back to you over and over again. It causes you to feel small and insignificant, like a failure and a nuisance. It is that little voice that chants, "I told you so!" In essence, the ego is one part of your being that seems to enjoy keeping you low. It speaks to you in a way you would never speak to anyone else.

You are the one person you can never get away from. It is so easy to punish yourself for what happened to you. It is so easy to believe that it was your fault because nothing else makes any sense. It is so easy to spew all the hatred and anger you feel right back at yourself because you feel incapable of spewing those words into the face of the person who deserves them the most.

But the ego does not have to talk to you like that. The ego can also purr like a kitten and pat itself on the back for a job well done, which, in turn, will make you feel exhilarated. It is possible! But you have to train it to behave in this manner. Just as you can choose to talk negatively to yourself through your ego, you can choose to lift yourself up through your ego. Yes, it is a choice. It is your choice whether you see rain as a tragedy or a blessing. You can choose to see a hot day as too hot to handle or as an opportunity to enjoy the pool, the beach, or a walk in the woods. The choice is yours. All it takes is that first baby step toward adjusting your mindset.

Let me ask you something: Deep down, do you really believe all of the negative things your ego tells you about yourself? Maybe there is one part of yourself that says, ever so faintly, "Wait a minute. That is not true! I am not a failure! I am not ugly! I am not a horrible person! I did not deserve this! I am lovable! I just have to be!"

One of the major obstacles we face is that we have been trained by generations of people whose minds were focused on hardship and despair, believing in the negative rather than the positive. According to them, the negative is reality, and the positive is merely wishful thinking. To that, I say, "Rubbish!"

Let's get back to that little positive voice that doubts your ego ever so slightly. This voice comes from your heart. Did you know that the heart has synapses and neurons, just like the brain? In essence, it is your second brain. Your heart-brain. It has just recently been discovered that the heart is constructed remarkably similar to the brain, and it sends signals throughout the body. So, in essence this means that when you follow your heart, you literally think through your heart. Isn't that fascinating?

You can train your ego to listen to your heart rather than your brain. You can train your ego to come from a place of compassion and kindness. You have all of these qualities within you. They are just buried underneath all of the pain, traumatic memories, and fears.

Essentially, you have been taught to focus your attention on the negative rather than the positive. This, in turn, causes you to be afraid of stepping out of your comfort zone, as the ego could not handle a positive outcome, and so it creates horror scenarios in your mind in order to scare you away from challenging yourself.

In the past chapter, I encouraged you to challenge your routine, and I am now encouraging you to challenge what you believe about yourself.

Let's take self-loathing for example. If you feel you are ugly, unlovable, that means you have issues with self-love. This can stem from so many different sources. It could be as simple as a boy you had a crush on in school telling you that you were ugly and that he wanted nothing to do with you. Or it could come from sexual abuse or any other type of trauma.

Regardless of the source, the approach is the same. In order to feel lovable, you have to first love yourself.

Here is an exercise that may weird you out at first, but I highly recommend that you give it a try. I am talking about "mirror work." Mirror work means that you look at yourself in the mirror and tell yourself something loving and encouraging, or even complimentary. You could start off with something like this:

In the morning, when you get up and go to the bathroom, on the way to the toilet, look at yourself in the mirror and say, "Good morning, sunshine." And smile at yourself. Do that every morning for a week and see what happens. Maybe you notice that it gives you a jolt of happiness when you hear those words while looking at yourself. Then you can add to this new-found routine. As you get ready for work, you could say something like, "Wow! You look so beautiful today! That outfit really suits you." Or be a little sassy: "Damn, girl, don't you look dashing today!" Or if you have an important meeting or presentation, you could say something like, "You got this, girl! I believe in you!"

If you continue this practice for a while, you will notice a change within you. You will look forward to the mornings when you greet yourself. You will love those moments because you will begin to feel uplifted, and you will begin to notice how this changes your mood for the whole day. You'll begin to feel happy.

Here is what happens in the brain when you do positive self-talk. With each thought, action, and reaction, you create a new synopsis in the brain. New pathways. New brain cells. And with these new connections, you are literally rewiring your brain. (This is the science of neuroplasticity.) And with that, you are syncing your brain up with your heart. You're bringing both brains into unison. And after that, your ego follows.

I encourage you to try this mirror-work exercise and journal every day about how it makes you feel. In the beginning, it may feel weird, not right, or just silly. Don't listen to those thoughts. Challenge yourself. Do it anyway. Push through that ego-driven barrier that tells you that it is not going to work, that it is stupid, and that it has no merit. Do it anyway! And if you like, send me a message and tell me about it.

Notes:

How Can I Ever Trust Again?

I have heard this question more times than I can count: How can I ever trust someone again? I've heard people say, "Whenever I open up to someone, they disappoint or hurt me. Is everyone just out to get me? Will I ever find someone who just loves me for me? Will I ever find someone who is not a narcissist?" The list of questions could go on and on. It is truly heartbreaking when my clients come to me, completely defeated by their pasts and their many attempts to have one good day, and ask one or all of these questions.

The thing is, yes, you can learn to trust again. You can find someone who loves you just the way you are. You can find someone who will be loving, kind, compassionate, and supportive.

It all starts with you. It always starts with you. The concept is quite simple: What you send out, you will attract. What you believe, you will receive. What you focus on, you will create more of. Yin and yang. The law of attraction.

To be able to find someone who loves you for who you are, you have to begin by loving yourself for who you are. If you want someone in your life who respects you and your choices, you have to first respect yourself and stop second-guessing every move you make. This sounds quite logical in theory, but actually practicing this can pose a challenge.

As with every other aspect of trauma healing and releasing old, destructive patterns, you have to practice diligent self-reflection. You have to become comfortable with analyzing yourself and learn from your behavior. You have to be completely non-judgmental toward yourself and accept and love yourself without prejudice. You simply have to love yourself, accept where you are on your journey at this very moment, and give yourself time to release.

In a previous chapter, I wrote that you can be your own worst enemy, your greatest critic, and your meanest friend. Now you must challenge yourself to become your best friend, your most enthusiastic cheerleader, and the greatest love of your life. You have to have compassion for yourself. You have to accept where you are at. Don't be afraid to look into the deepest, darkest depths of your being. It is because of the darkness that you can see the light.

To release what needs releasing, you have to approach your darkness by focusing on the light you can see behind it. The darkness within you is nothing more than an obstacle in your path to joy, peace, and happiness. I said it before, and I will say it again: Trauma is not a life sentence. All you need to do is choose to release it. You have to choose to not be held hostage by it any longer. You have to choose not to see yourself as your past. You have to choose life over existence.

You are worthy of receiving everything you dream of. You are worthy of creating the life you want, but you have to first believe that you are worthy of it. If you doubt yourself constantly, if you loathe yourself, if you body-shame yourself, or if you self-sabotage, you first have to heal the aspects of yourself that cause these behaviors and limiting beliefs.

You have to break the cycle and reinvent yourself from the bottom up.

As I write this, I am thinking to myself: This is so unfair! At first, we were forced to endure these traumatic incidences, and now we have to completely overhaul ourselves because of it. And yes, it is easy to fall into this mindset. But look at it from a different perspective: You had to experience something truly horrible, and you are still here. You managed to pull yourself back up. That proves how incredibly strong and resilient you are! Now take that strength and resilience and change your life for the better! Thrive, not despite of it all, but because of it! What does not break you makes you stronger. And the trauma did not break you! It merely redirected you for a while.

The Complexity of Guilt

Guilt is a very complex emotion that can keep you hostage within yourself for the rest of your life. In this chapter, I will touch on the concept of guilt and forgiveness. I will be talking about a situation where a person does feel guilty yet seeks forgiveness, and I will discuss a situation where a person chooses to forgive even though an apology will most likely never come. Lastly, I will talk about how important it is to forgive yourself.

What if You Are the One Who Has to Forgive?

Let's say you have been hurt very badly by someone else. You were hurt by their betrayal, by their wrongful accusations and actions, or by this person simply not having your back when you needed this person the most. What should you do if you know that you will most likely never receive an apology? Most likely, you will cut that person out of your life. And then what? The wound this person caused is still festering within you. In your mind, you keep going back to that dreadful situation, and you feel hurt all over again.

I was in a situation like this not too long ago, and I can tell you that it was not pretty. But I had a choice to make. I had to decide whether I wanted to stubbornly wait for an apology that would most likely never come or whether I was willing to forgive that person for my own sake and move on. I chose forgiveness. Does it still hurt? Yes, it does, but that is my own pain and trauma that I have to deal with. It does not involve the other person.

Holding a grudge does not help you. It just keeps you in a state of constant unhappiness. Forgiving someone else is the most powerful choice you can make for yourself and your own well-being. To forgive someone for her actions does not mean that you have to tell her. Your choice to forgive this person has nothing to do with her. It has everything to do with yourself.

What if You Are Seeking Forgiveness?

Asking someone for forgiveness can feel hard and uncomfortable. The worst part is not knowing whether that person will accept your apology.

Many people do not apologize because they feel too ashamed about their actions and fear having their apology rejected. They themselves do not feel deserving of forgiveness. Others may cope with their guilt by simply not acknowledging that they did something wrong and acting oblivious to the opinions of others. Others may believe that they were in the right and that there is no need for them to apologize.

A heartfelt and sincere apology should always be enough. But what if your apology is not accepted?

Whatever a person's reason is for not accepting your apology, it has nothing to do with you. It simply means that she is not ready to face her own pain and let the incident go. However, even though this person did not forgive you, you are still allowed to let it go and make peace with yourself. Unfortunately, though, many people continue to feel guilty because they make their own happiness conditional on the forgiveness of the other person. That is not necessary at all.

You acknowledged that you did something wrong, and you had the courage to apologize. This means that you did all you could do and are now allowed to move on. It is not your responsibility to feel guilty until the other person is ready to heal. On the contrary, by continuing to feel guilty, you may actually hinder the other person from moving on.

What if You Are Unable to Forgive Yourself?

Forgiving someone else may seem difficult, but it is not nearly as difficult as forgiving yourself. You are always your own worst critic. You expect perfection from yourself even though you may not expect the same from others. So, when you do something you perceive as wrong, you might end up punishing yourself over and over again. You keep going back to that moment and reliving it again and again. To make matters worse, with each passing year that you feel guilty, your mind will exacerbate the incident.

You can forgive someone else while still choosing to keep him or her out of your life, but you can't run from yourself. When you feel guilty or ashamed about something you did, something you didn't do and should have, something you did not try hard enough to prevent, or something you are being told you should feel guilty about, you have to remind yourself that you are just as worthy of forgiveness as anyone else. But sadly, that is not always enough.

So how can we forgive someone we can't ever get away from? The very fact that you do feel guilty shows that you are full of remorse. Remorse is a sign that you have compassion for the other person. But what if the person you hurt already forgave you, yet you still can't forgive yourself? What if you believe that you are not worthy of forgiveness?

The thing is, the more compassionate you are, the harder it is to forgive yourself for hurting another person. As a compassionate person, failing someone you care about is one of the worst things you could ever do according to your own mind. Yet it is you who is most deserving of forgiveness.

To forgive yourself, you have to acknowledge that you are keeping yourself hostage through your guilt. Then you have to ask yourself why you don't allow yourself to let it go, because in most cases, this amplified feeling of guilt has a completely different source.

This kind of self-reflection is extremely difficult, especially when you are trapped in your own negative mindset. Therefore, I would suggest seeking help in the form of counseling, coaching, or holistic practices in order to release the guilt and any paralyzing emotion that is attached to it.

However, if you feel guilt or shame, you may feel unable to open up about your pain to someone else, as the guilt is just too great. If this is how you, or someone you know, feel, please remember that in order to heal, you have to step out of your comfort zone. I know all too well that opening up about pain is a huge step, but I also know that it is the most necessary one, and the most rewarding.

Why Choose Forgiveness?

Why choose forgiveness? This one simple question will undoubtedly trigger many of you, and understandably so. When you hear the word forgiveness, you probably automatically go into defense mode, especially when it is related to deep trauma.

So many times, I have seen the facial expression of a client change as soon as I mention the word forgiveness. A tender, loving person can transform into a bloodthirsty, battle-ready Viking warrior right in front of my eyes. I can see the spite, the hate, the pain, the anger, and, yes, even the panic rushing to the surface.

- He does not deserve my forgiveness! I wish he would rot in hell!
- I will never forgive her!
- Why should I forgive him? He did not see anything wrong with his behavior!
- People like her do not deserve to be forgiven.

I get that. I really do. I have been there. I've said the exact same words. I've felt the same hatred toward my abusers. Forgiveness, for me, was out of the question. I wanted revenge!

When you resent forgiveness, it is not just out of anger. There is much more going on. You resent forgiveness because you are deeply hurt. You know that you will never receive an apology, you know that your abuser will most likely never face justice, and you know there will be no retribution. You are in pain because the wrong that was dealt to you will never be righted. And of course, there is that infamous underlying fear of what other people may think.

But what if forgiveness meant something entirely different from what you believe it to be? What if forgiveness meant freeing yourself from this emotional prison? What if it meant liberty for your soul? What if you did not make forgiveness about your abuser? What if you actually made it about yourself? What if forgiveness meant that you allowed yourself to be released from this toxic connection?

How about, rather than calling it forgiveness, we call it something else? How about we call it seeking freedom, separation from trauma, or simply letting go?

Processing the very idea of forgiveness will bring many emotions to the surface. After the spite, the hate, the pain, the anger, and the panic have subsided, another set of said emotions will flood into your consciousness.

When I ask people why they won't forgive, every answer and reason I get is fueled by an incredible amount of pain, shame, helplessness, and gut-wrenching fear. I get questions like:

- If I forgive, won't that make my trauma insignificant?
- If I forgive, can I no longer say that my traumatic event happened?
- If I forgive, will I have to say that I am okay with what happened?
- If I forgive, what will my friends say? Will they see me as weak?
- If I forgive, does that mean I should drop the charges?
- Who am I without it?

I am sure you will have similar thoughts popping into your mind while reading this. And the answer to each and every one of these thoughts and questions is no. Not one of those statements is factual, but it's easy to see why you, a trauma survivor, would believe they are. So many survivors of abuse and trauma get stuck in the "anger phase" out of fear of letting go. They struggle with the belief that letting it go will minimize the incident. This is not true! The incident won't lose its severity. It will always be the same incident, but you won't be held hostage by it anymore, and you can move on with your life.

What happened to you is a part of your life story. It will always remain a part of your life story. But you can refuse to allow it to have control over you. That's what's important!

Just because someone else chose to abuse you, does not mean you have to punish yourself for it by not releasing it.

TRAUMA IS NOT A LIFE SENTENCE.

Allowing yourself to let go of the trauma you had to experience does not make the incident irrelevant. What you were put through is inexcusable. Letting go means you won't allow it to hold you hostage any longer.

Why is forgiveness so important? Why can't you just stay angry about what happened and move on with your life? Well, the truth is, as long as you are angry, there is no moving on. You may tell yourself that you moved on, but that is just an illusion.

Not too long ago, when I talked about forgiveness in a Facebook group, one woman wrote, "I will never forgive him for what he did. He does not deserve my forgiveness. I left the past behind me and moved on. I am over it. And I am fine." Does that sound like moving on to you? It certainly does not to me. It sounds more like suppressing than releasing.

The thing is, when you are angry, you are basically punishing yourself for something that someone else did or said. You are angry because you were wronged, and you know that you will most likely never receive an apology or retribution. You are angry because you have been mistreated, abused, disrespected, and shamed.

And anger is a valid emotion. There is no doubt about it. It is okay to be angry. But if you hold on to anger too long, it can take control over you. This means you went from one extreme to the next. At first, the trauma controlled you. And now that you have finally taken back control, you're allowing the anger to take over. Holding on to anger can cause many issues:

- You can become bitter and resentful, not just against your abuser, but against anyone who you feel has wronged you.
- You can be easily triggered.
- You may begin to react aggressively against anyone you believe has done something to hurt you.
- You may blame everyone else for how you feel.

That is not letting go. That is holding on to your anger and punishing others for it, which can rather quickly turn you into the abuser.

The other important aspect to consider is that as long as you are angry or resentful toward your abuser, you have an emotional connection with that person. Let's call it an energetic bond. By refusing to forgive and release the anger, you will forever have that connection, which will cause you to feel angry about what happened over and over again. That is a lot of negativity to hold on to.

If you instead choose to release your abuser from your body, mind, and soul, you will also release yourself from that emotional connection.

Forgiveness, in this case, does not mean forgiving what happened to you; it just means releasing your attacker from your bondage. Because, just as you force yourself to stay energetically connected to your attacker, he or she is also energetically connected to you. You both constantly receive energy from each other, even if you are not in each other's lives any longer. In this way, you are still giving your abuser control over you.

Wouldn't it be better to dislodge yourself from this toxic bond? And with that, free yourself? In essence, you would choose to reduce your attacker to no more than an insignificant speck of dust that is floating in a beam of sunlight. A speck of dust that has no meaning whatsoever in your life.

One thing I would like to add is that society has taught you to never forgive, as abuse does not deserve forgiveness. At some point in your healing journey, you will come to question this belief, and it may even go so far as to create inner turmoil within yourself. One part of you may want to forgive and truly let go, and the other part may feel the need to continue to be angry at what happened because society demands it.

But it does not have to be so. You create your own world. One person sees rain as a tragedy; another sees it as a blessing. It is all in the mindset. What society says or wants has nothing to do with you. You are an individual; you are not society. So, choose what kind of life you want to live and then take the first step toward it by releasing the past.

Forgiveness may seem like the most challenging aspect of trauma healing, but it is by far the most rewarding. It allows you to be truly free of your past.

- Forgiveness means that you choose to leave your past behind.
- Forgiveness means that you won't be ruled by what happened to you.
- Forgiveness means that you are stronger than your circumstances.

Can you imagine how much courage it takes to choose forgiveness? To be the person who walks away and never looks back?

Like I said before and will continue to say over and over again throughout this book: When it comes to trauma, you are the one who is not allowing yourself to move on. You are the one who is holding yourself hostage. If you choose forgiveness, you are opening the doors to your self-created prison cell, walking through them, and, for the first time in a very long time, feeling the sun shine on your face and the wind brush against you. You see the world in a whole new light. It's no longer a dark and dingy prison; it's a bright new world full of wonder, opportunity, and freedom.

Exercise and Guided Meditation:

Getting to the point where you are ready to forgive, release the past, and let go of the people who hurt you is a journey. You will know when you are ready. You will notice that the craving to be free and at peace with what happened is outweighing the need for anger and resentment. Once you are ready, I invite you to follow this guided meditation.

Before we begin, I want to point out a few things. The steps I am listing below may not resonate with you. If you are afraid of water, then of course you would not feel comfortable envisioning yourself standing in a lake, right? So, if that is the case, then choose a scenery that makes you the most comfortable and at peace. Use the outline below as a general guide and adjust the mental image to your liking. You can even create your own version by writing down the meditation below but adjusting it to the image you feel drawn to using.

You can repeat this meditation as often as you like. Sometimes it takes a couple of tries before you can truly release someone.

Let's begin with my favorite grounding meditation. This will allow you to release negative energy and ground yourself before going deeper.

- Choose your favorite meditation music.
- Sit comfortably with your feet firmly on the ground.
- Close your eyes and breathe deeply. Let the air fill your lungs completely, and as your lungs get full, breathe in even more air and slowly

fill your stomach. Hold your breath for a brief moment and then slowly release it. Repeat two or three times.

- Breathe in for four seconds, hold your breath for four seconds, and breathe out for eight seconds. Repeat two or three times.

- Now imagine thick, gnarly roots that come out of the soles of your feet and grow deep into the ground until they reach the center of the Earth.

- At the center of the Earth is a river. Imagine that your roots keep growing until their tips touch the water.

- Breathe in deeply, and as you breathe in, imagine that you collect all of the negative and excess energy in the center of your core.

- As you breathe out, imagine that this energy is being pushed down your body, through your feet and into the roots. The energy will flow down your roots and into the water, and then it will be washed away by the river.

- Repeat four to five times until all of the negative energy is gone.

- Imagine a ball of golden healing energy forming at your roots and moving up into your body, through your body, and out at the top of your head, connecting you with the divine source.

Guided Meditation for Letting Go of People:

- Choose your favorite meditation music.
- Close your eyes and take a deep breath. Feel all of the stress and worry leave you.
- Picture yourself standing at the shore of a shallow lake in the light of the full moon. You can see silhouettes of trees on the shoreline, and even some in the water. See the reflection of the moon shimmering on the lake. The air smells sweet and inviting. You are at peace. You feel drawn to the water and begin to walk into the lake. Even though it is night, the water is not cold. You find it rather refreshing. As you walk, you can feel how the water is cleansing your body, mind, and soul of the pain of the past. With each step you take, you feel lighter, more at peace.
- You continue walking until the water comes to your knees.
- As you stand in the smooth ebb and flow of the lake, you feel the tingle of the moonlight washing over you.
- You sense that you are no longer alone and look around. You see that you are surrounded by your angels, guides,

ancestors, and spirit animals. You feel at peace, protected, and loved.

- You now tell your angels, guides, ancestors, and spirit animals that you wish to release the past and everyone who hurt you from your body, mind, and soul, and you ask for their assistance. Your angels, guides, ancestors, and spirit animals smile at you encouragingly and send you feelings of love, hope, and peace.

- Feel these emotions as they wash over you and become a part of you.

- Focus on the trees you can see on the shoreline in front of you and call forth the person or people you wish to release. See them coming toward you. Do not be afraid. They can't hurt you.

- As you see that person standing a few feet away from you, imagine an energetic bond connecting the two of you. Envision it like a cord that is attached to both of you.

- As you look at that person, take the cord that is attached to you and gently remove it from your body. Imagine how it easily detaches from your soul, and then release it into the water. See it dissolving into hundreds of specks of light and watch it being washed away by the gentle waves of the lake.

- Envision that person fading away as you say, "I release you."
- Feel how your angels, guides, ancestors, and spirit animals touch you on your shoulder and send you their love and peace, which fills the void that was created after you released this person from your body, mind, and soul.
- Thank your angels, guides, ancestors, and spirit animals for their assistance. Take one last deep breath and walk out of the lake back to the shoreline.
- When you are ready, take a deep breath and open your eyes.

Repeat this meditation with anyone you wish to release.

The Emotional Hangover

When you are releasing emotions, beliefs, and whatever else keeps you stuck, you have to understand that the emotions that used to be buried will have to come up to be released.

Let's say that you just had a coaching session with me, and it resulted in an incredible a-ha moment. The a-ha moment is the moment when you have a profound realization. This realization will create a shift within you.

It is truly fascinating. After you have this a-ha moment, the limiting belief you had begins to shift and leave your body. It is no longer needed. That ground-breaking moment can make you feel like you're bubbling over with excitement, freedom, and joy. It may feel as if a huge weight has been lifted off your shoulders.

But as we all know, every high is followed by a low. In this case, however, it is actually a good low. So, here is the thing: When you have a huge shift within yourself, you are automatically releasing the negative emotions attached to that now-outdated belief system. The negative emotions have to come to the surface of your consciousness to be released. There is no other way.

When you experience a positive shift one day, you will most likely feel down, worn out, sad, depressed, angry, frustrated, or just plain negative during the following days. You may wonder what just happened. Yesterday, you felt incredible, and today you are all doom and despair. Please understand that this is normal! You are releasing the energy that is no longer needed and the emotions that are no longer valid.

Do not suppress these emotions. Just acknowledge them and let them work their way out of your system. You will feel much better the next day.

When you first begin your journey into trauma healing, those emotional hangovers, as I like to call them, can be pretty intense. But rest assured that they will always pass. You might assume that when you feel a certain way, it is because of outside influences, but that is not true in most cases. Whatever you feel, especially after a positive shift, comes from within. It has to come up. I can not stress this enough: It has to come up to be released.

It will pass, and you will feel so much better afterward.

"Our sorrows and wounds are healed

only when we touch them with compassion."

—Buddha

Grounding 101

My grandparents used to say that I should stop dreaming and stand with both feet on the ground. They meant that I should not chase dreams that will never come true; instead, I should focus on the here and now, be responsible, and find a job that pays the bills.

They weren't wrong.

If you want to achieve your goals, you have to have your head in the game and have a plan. Sweet talk and daydreaming won't get you to where you want to go. That is not to say that dreaming about your goals and having them come to life in your mind is not important. To be successful, it is crucial for you to be able to envision your ultimate goal in all of its glory.

Now, what does that have to do with grounding? Quite a bit, actually. Grounding is a state of being that is greatly influenced by your thoughts, your actions, and your environment. When you are grounded, you feel calm, balanced, and ready to take on the world. You stand, unwavering, and feel comfortable with who you are at that very moment. You are confident about your goals and the road toward them.

When you are ungrounded, you may feel anxious, nervous, and full of doubts and fears. Your goal seems so far out of reach, and the road ahead is too uncertain for comfort. Being ungrounded can be the reason you fail in an important moment.

Whether you are grounded or ungrounded has a lot to do with your root chakra. The root chakra sits at the base of your spine and symbolizes your energetic, vibrational, and spiritual foundation. Even though your chakra system is considered a solely spiritual aspect of you, it has an immense influence on your overall health and well-being. (I will go more into detail about grounding and the chakras in the following chapter.)

When you are ungrounded, it will amplify your limiting beliefs, your self-sabotaging behavior, and your self-imposed blockages. At the same time, your limiting beliefs, self-sabotaging behavior, and self-imposed blockages can cause the ungroundedness. It is a vicious cycle.

When I am ungrounded, I tend to start one chore, then suddenly stop and start another one, only to desert that and go back to the first or even a third one. I tend to run around like a headless chicken. Then I usually get irritated very easily. Any and all disturbances drive me up the wall. Basically, when I am ungrounded, I am stressed, agitated, anxious, and, frankly, not very good company. And that is on a good day of being ungrounded.

On a bad day of being ungrounded, I feel completely overwhelmed by everything that is going on in my life. I have serious self-doubt about my path and stress over every aspect of it. I may become terrified of a public-speaking engagement or live interview. Fear of rejection is my last major limiting belief. And when I am ungrounded, it is even more prominent in my mind, body, and soul.

When I am grounded, it is quite the opposite. I feel balanced, happy, and excited about things as they unfold. I cook, I clean, and I sing while doing it. When I am grounded, I think of my fears and just say, "Bring it on!" When I am grounded, I have a solid foundation.

There are many wonderful ways to ground yourself. I will talk about some in the following chapters, and I encourage you to test them all. See which one you like the best. You can, of course, also use different techniques or combine some. There is no right or wrong way to ground yourself once you understand the principles.

How do you get ungrounded? Let's say you have a big meeting at work. You have your one big shot at presenting a project that has been your baby for many months. You wake up in the morning and think, Oh no! Today, I have to speak in front of management and everyone on my team about my project. Even though you are very well prepared, and you know your project inside and out, fear creeps into your mind. Fear of failing, fear of judgment, and fear of rejection. And boom! You are ungrounded. You may literally feel as if someone just pulled the rug out from underneath you. You start to feel stressed, anxious, and nervous.

All of these feelings stem from ungroundedness. Now, if you know that feeling and know the cause, it is very easy to ground yourself before going to work. The meeting will most likely go over smoothly, and you'll get through it without the anxiety you would normally have. But if you don't understand the cause of that feeling, you will get more anxious and stressed throughout the day. You will make it through the meeting and then worry for the rest of the day if your management liked what they heard.

It is easy to get ungrounded, and it is just as simple to get grounded again.

How do you know when you are ungrounded?

Grounding and The Chakras

As with everything in life, balance is key. If there is an imbalance within you, you may conclude that continuous grounding will bring you relief. But that is not necessarily true. You can also become too grounded; in which case you might feel as if you are dragging your feet through sticky mud while having weights attached to your ankles.

Being too grounded means that the lower chakras are spinning while at least one of the upper chakras is not.

There are many more aspects to being ungrounded than just not being grounded. Let's take a look at your breathing as an example. When you are anxious or are experiencing a lot of stress, you generally breathe very shallowly. If you breathe shallowly, the breath doesn't reach your lower chakras. Breathing shallowly causes an imbalance, especially when it is accompanied by feelings of stress, anxiety, or fear. This, in itself, can cause your root chakra to slow down or stop spinning.

Have you ever practiced yoga or meditation? Even if you haven't, you have probably seen or heard about how, at the beginning of each session, you are asked to take a deep breath. This deep breath has the power to release negative or excess energy and align all of your seven chakras.

So, let's recap: When you are feeling anxious, stressed, or overwhelmed, this mainly involves the upper chakras. Everything that makes your heart flutter, constricts your breathing, or messes with your mind is related to the heart chakra, throat chakra, third eye chakra, and crown chakra, and it usually means that at least one of the lower chakras—meaning the root chakra, sacral chakra, or solar plexus chakra—is out of alignment.

On the other hand, when you are feeling depressed, have extremely low self-esteem, or just have a doomsday attitude, this involves the lower chakras. Everything that drags you down is related to either the root, sacral, or solar plexus chakra. And in this case, at least one of the upper chakras is out of alignment.

As you can see, your mood can be greatly influenced by your chakras. If your chakras are not "healthy," it causes an imbalance within you. This imbalance can be mild, like feeling a bit overwhelmed at times, or it can be severe, like a panic attack. What you are feeling and experiencing on a mental/emotional level can be linked back to the health of your chakras.

Grounding does not only mean rooted in the earth. The counterpart, the attachment to heaven, also has to be present in order for you to achieve the balanced feeling of being grounded. Through the root chakra, you are grounded in the lower realms, and through the crown chakra you are rooted in the higher realms. If you are grounding yourself and all of your chakras are open and spinning, this balance is created automatically. As above, so below. Picture the yin and yang symbol. Perfect balance.

When you believe that you need to ground yourself because you feel anxious, there may be an imbalance in one of your lower chakras. Grounding alone won't fix this in the long run. Grounding can help as a temporary solution. Even though it may make you feel balanced and whole again, the chakra in question will continue to act up until you address the underlying issue.

When you notice something is wrong, focus your attention inward and focus on which chakra is not working as it should be. To do that, especially when you have never focused on your chakras before, pull up an image of their associated colors online and focus your attention on each one individually. You will begin at your root chakra and end with your crown chakra. You may feel a dull ache or pressure, slight nausea, or congestion in the affected area. Just trust your intuition.

When it comes to trauma healing, being grounded is key. When you experienced trauma, you literally lost your foundation, which means your lower chakras are most likely blocked. This is especially true with sexual assault and rape. The root chakra is your foundation. The sacral chakra is connected to your sexuality. The solar plexus chakra has to do with your self-esteem and willpower.

We will look deeper into the chakras, how to check their openness, and how to align them in the next section of this book. For now, let's focus on how to ground.

Exercise: Unless you have been trained as a singer or a dancer or you practice meditation or yoga, chances are, you are not breathing as you should be. Therefore, let's practice it. Focus on your breathing. Notice whether you breathe into your stomach or into your chest. Try to consciously breathe deeply into your stomach and take note of how you feel after taking a few breaths.

____

____

____

____

____

____

____

____

Different Grounding Techniques

Let's look at a number of different grounding methods. It is important to understand that intention is key! Whatever exercise you choose, do it with intent. You can set your intention before you begin by simply stating out loud, or in your mind, "I am now grounding myself."

Also, don't forget your breathing. Take deep, slow breaths in and out during the entire exercise. Shallow breathing won't give you the same results.

Grounding in Nature:

Being in nature is a wonderful way to ground yourself and release excess and negative energy. Simply take off your shoes and walk on the grass, on the beach, or in the woods. Or sit in your garden, close your eyes, and let nature do its magic. Mother Nature has a way of removing your negative energy and replenishing your reserves.

If you are not too keen on walking barefoot outside, look for a tree. Oak trees, in particular, are wonderful grounding agents. Lean your back against the tree and press your hands onto the bark. Close your eyes and feel the ancient energy of this wonderful being rush through you. If you feel comfortable with this method, why not say hello to the tree? You can start an energetic conversation. Trees can tell you a lot of stories from times long past. I know that this is not for everyone, and that is perfectly fine. We all feel drawn to many different things and beings, and for some of us, it's trees.

Gardening is another wonderful way to ground yourself. Digging in the dirt and giving your flowers and shrubs room to grow is not only satisfying, but it's also very grounding, especially if you do it consciously.

How did you experience grounding in nature? Write down your experiences below:

____

____

____

____

____

____

____

____

____

____

The Chi, Ki, Prana Method:

Stand with both feet firmly on the ground. Close your eyes and take a deep breath. While you breathe in, stretch your arms out, palms up, to either side of your body, and then lift them over your head and place your hands together. As you breathe out, lower your joined hands until they come to rest in front of your heart, your fingers pointing upward.

Keep your hands in this position for the duration of this grounding exercise. This position is not only to center yourself, but it's also to connect the left and right sides of your brain. If you do this motion consciously, you can actually feel the connection.

Move your focus inward, to the point right behind your navel. This is where the source of your Ki, Chi, or Prana (your life force energy) resides. Imagine that in the center of your body, behind your navel, is a ball of golden light. Focus on this spot for a few seconds. Intentionally focusing your attention on your Chi will almost instantly ground you.

Notes:

____

____

____

____

The Breathing Method:

Sit comfortably. Close your eyes and take a deep breath. Let the air fill your lungs completely, and when your lungs are full, breathe in even more air and guide it through your diaphragm and into your stomach. When your stomach is full, hold your breath for four to five seconds and then slowly breathe out. While you breathe in, you can imagine that you're drawing all of the negative and excess energy into your stomach, and by breathing out you release it with your breath. Repeat until you feel calm and balanced.

This exercise is also very helpful when you suffer from constipation. To help with that, breathe in deeply and focus on moving your bowels along with every breath out. You may have to do the breathing for a few minutes, but be patient, and it will work.

Notes:

____

____

____

____

____

____

____

____

____

____

____

____

____

____

____

____

The Root Method:

Stand tall, your feet firmly on the ground. Close your eyes and imagine you have roots coming out from the soles of your feet, extending deep into the ground and into the core of the Earth. Now imagine that all of the excess energy is flowing down your body, through the roots, and into the Earth. When you feel that all of the negative energy has been guided into the Earth, imagine that golden healing energy is coming up from the core of the Earth, through the roots, into your feet, and extending throughout your body. Imagine that this healing energy surrounds you and fills every void or crack the negative energy left behind.

When you feel that you are filled and surrounded by golden healing energy, imagine that the roots detach from your feet and dissolve into the ground.

Notes:

The Emergency Method 1:

The emergency methods are great when you need to ground instantly, or when you are among people who should not know what you are doing.

Focus on the soles of your feet. Just hold your mind there for a few seconds and relax. Then let that thought go. Focusing on your feet can ground you instantly. But remember, intention is key.

Notes:

The Emergency Method 2:

Push your index finger against your navel and push hard into your stomach. This will instantly ground you. By pushing your stomach inward at the point of your naval, you will connect to your Chi.

Notes:

The Connection Method:

Stand up firmly, your feet parallel to each other. Imagine a line going over your head from one ear to the other. Now envision another line going from your third eye to the back of your head, crossing the line connecting both of your ears. See the connection where the two lines cross at the top of your skull, above your crown chakra, and envision a cord extending into heaven, connecting you with the divine.

Now envision a line that connects the soles of your feet. In the middle of this line, another one forms that leads deep down to the center of the Earth. Hold this image for a few seconds. You are now connected to heaven and Earth.

Now imagine that healing energy from heaven is descending down into your body and surrounding you. And by extending into your body, the healing energy slowly moves the negative, excess energy down your body, into your feet, and down the cord leading into the Earth. Once you feel that you are completely balanced and at peace, retract the cords.

Notes:

____
____
____
____
____
____
____
____
____
____
____
____
____

There are, of course, many more wonderful grounding techniques. Why don't you create your own?

My favorite grounding technique:

Grounding Colors

Do you recall the last time you went shopping and browsed through the clothing section? Did you find yourself leaning toward a specific color? No matter where you looked, without fail, could you always find that one specific shade you had in your mind? And let's say you went shopping again a few months later. Were you then drawn to a completely different color?

Many people believe that their taste in color has just changed over time. But is that really all there is to it? What if I told you that the colors you feel drawn to are giving you insight into what you are currently working through on a spiritual, mental, or emotional level? And what if I told you that the colors you feel drawn to are the vibrational support you need in order to resolve those issues you are currently working through?

Colors play a huge role in every aspect of your life. Just think about logos. The colors in a logo are selected to bring forth a specific emotion. Many scientific studies have been conducted on the use of color and the emotional reaction. This is truly fascinating because it shows that colors have their own vibration and that, depending on your own needs, you will resonate more with one color than another. This phenomenon is directly linked to your chakras. Each chakra is associated with a specific color. Depending on what you are working through on a spiritual, mental, or emotional level, at least one of the seven chakras is affected. Therefore, you always feel drawn to the color that is associated with that specific chakra.

Let's say that you are working on being more outspoken, which means you are subconsciously releasing a pattern that stopped you from speaking up or speaking your mind. In this case, you would be drawn to colors associated with the throat chakra, which are various shades of blue. If you were now releasing old pattern behaviors that had to do with self-love or allowing others to truly love you, then you would work with the heart chakra, whose colors are shades of either green or pink.

Once you become more in tune with your body and energy, your body will often tell you which chakra needs your attention by focusing your mind on a specific color.

As stated earlier, your root chakra is the one through which you become grounded, which means, to consciously ground, you must focus on colors associated with the root chakra. The colors for grounding are earthy colors, which makes perfect sense. Any shade of black, red, or brown is grounding. If you feel that you are in need of some grounding, wear a red scarf or some black pants and a black shirt and put them on with the intention of being grounded that day. You will notice that you feel more balanced, calmer, and your life will seem less chaotic.

Having intention is key. By deciding that you are wearing a specific piece of clothing with the intention of grounding yourself, you're turning a key and opening a door. The intention allows the grounding energy to flow through your body and ground you.

Notes:

Grounding Crystals

I have met quite a few people who have an array of crystals at home, and each day they intuitively pick a couple to carry with them. I find this to be a wonderful practice, and if you resonate with it, why not give it a shot?

To start your crystal collection, visit a crystal store. You will see hundreds of different crystals. Some will look very alike, and others will be unlike any you have ever seen.

When it comes to crystals, size and shape do not really matter. What matters is what you feel drawn to. I generally feel drawn to the rough, unpolished crystals. But others prefer the little tumbled ones. Just go with your gut, and you can't go wrong. At the shop, let your eyes wander over all of the crystals a couple of times and take mental notes of the ones you feel an interest in. It could be as subtle as a little jolt or as unsubtle as a little tingle or shiver. Make sure you take the little information card so that you always know which crystal you just bought.

I highly recommend taking a picture of each of the crystals you purchased, including the card, and keep a file on your computer, or other device, for reference. You can even create your own little crystal bible by noting how you felt using a particular crystal, or you could add the online description of the crystal you felt most drawn to. Trust me, at some point in the future, you may be unsure about which crystal you are using. It is so easy to forget their names or mistake them for another one.

Keep your crystals in close proximity to your body. They need to be within your auric field to be effective. Placing them on your desk or in your purse is not close enough. You can, of course, have them in your purse and take them out when you feel drawn to hold, touch, or rub them. You can also place them on your chair, below your leg, or under your pillow.

Crystals can be a very helpful grounding tool. In general, any black, red, or brown crystal is grounding. Here is a list of a few wonderful grounding crystals:

- Black Tourmaline
- Black Obsidian
- Red Jasper
- Apache Tear
- Blood Stone
- Hematite (or Magnetite, which is Hematite, only magnetic)
- Carnelian
- Ruby

Let's talk about how to take care of your crystals. First of all, before you use them, they need to be cleansed. Crystals take on a lot of energy, especially when they are held.

The crystal you chose may have gone through hundreds of hands before it found its way to you.

This means that the residue of all of those different energies linger in the crystal. There are only two crystals in the world that do not hold on to energy and cleanse themselves: citrine and kyanite. All of the other crystals have to be cleansed on a regular basis, especially before first use.

To cleanse your crystals, I would recommend getting a selenite plate. They are fairly inexpensive depending on the size. You can find them in your local crystal shop or online at Amazon, eBay, Etsy, or other marketplaces. Simply place your crystals on the selenite plate overnight. I would suggest you do the same with any crystal jewelry you own.

Several of my jewelry clients reported that their bracelets literally exploded. This is quite an interesting phenomenon. As I have mentioned above, there are only two crystals that cleanse themselves: citrine and kyanite. All of the other crystals are absorbing energy from you, either to help you release it or to increase their own healing energy so they can replenish yours. In either case, they do not release the excess energy from within themselves. It just lingers. Over time, the energy will build up more and more, which forces the gemstone beads on a bracelet apart to the point that the stringing material can not withstand the pressure anymore, causing it to rip apart. So always cleanse your crystals and crystal jewelry.

Which crystals did you find to be most helpful with grounding?

Grounding Wellness

One of my favorite ways to remove negative energy and ground myself is a salt bath, or rather a salt foot bath. If you have the luxury of owning a comfortable bathtub, then you are in luck! Ours is still one of those terribly uncomfortable ones from the 70s. So I am hardly ever taking a bath. If you do not have a bathtub or don't like taking baths, you can do a salt foot bath. I will address both and tell you exactly how to do them, what ingredients you could/should add, and what else to look out for.

Let me tell you that I absolutely love a salt foot bath. As soon as I put my feet into the water, I feel the energy starting to drain out of me. My whole body tingles, and my root chakra vibrates. It is pure bliss.

Which salt should you use? Different sources will give you different advice. Technically, almost any salt would work. However, I do not recommend table salt, as it has no nutrients at all. You should at least use sea salt.

Epsom salt is also a common suggestion. Some people also like to mix Epsom with other salts, which is also fine. I personally prefer Himalayan pink salt because it is full of more nutrients and minerals than most other salts. All of these minerals and nutrients will be absorbed by your body while you bathe. This is a really good thing because you generally are deficient of at least some of these nutrients and minerals, and a salt bath with Himalayan Pink salt not only removes negative and excess energy, but it also replenishes these deficiencies. Whatever your body does not need, it will simply discard.

So, you see, choosing the perfect salt for you can help you in more ways than one. Therefore, I encourage you to do your research on the different salts that are available and choose the one that is right for you. Don't just go by what other people recommend. Follow your instinct and choose the salt you most resonate with.

If you want to take a salt bath, you should use two to four cups of salt. This sounds like a lot but think about how much salt is in the ocean and how much water you put into the bathtub. At first, you may want to try using two cups, and then if you feel up to it, increase the amount. Add a few drops of frankincense, sandalwood, lavender, or myrrh to your bath or foot bath. These essential oils are wonderful grounding agents.

Some people also add rose quartz, clear quartz, and black tourmaline to their baths. Before you add crystals, make sure that they will not get corroded from the salt or water. Different crystals have different densities. The selenite, for example, belongs to the sandstone family and would dilute in water. The clear quarts and rose quartz, on the other hand, are almost as hard as diamonds and could be buried in salt for cleansing.

If you like to make a weekly ritual out of a salt bath, maybe on a Friday evening after a long work week, why not add some candles and some meditative music?

After your salt bath, rinse yourself off to remove any salt from your body. If you have been swimming in the ocean before, you know how it starts to sting and itch if you don't shower afterward. The same is true for a salt bath.

If you prefer taking a salt foot bath, I would recommend using about a half cup to one full cup of salt. Just like with the bath, you can add essential oils, light candles, and listen to music. For either bath, I would recommend the duration be a minimum of fifteen minutes and a maximum of thirty minutes.

If you are in a rush but would still like to benefit from the cleansing properties of the salt, I would recommend a salt soap bar or a salt peeler. A salt scrub can easily be made at home. Pinterest is a wonderful place to find recipes and instructions. You can use these in the shower every day. However, I would not recommend using the soap bar directly on your body. Instead, you should use a washcloth, as the salt can be pretty rough on your skin.

Add your notes:

On the following lines, I encourage you to write down your experience from your first salt bath. Try to remember how you felt before and after, if you noticed anything during the salt bath or salt foot bath, etc.

____

____

____

____

____

____

____

____

____

____

____

My Favorite Grounding Exercise

The following grounding exercise is my favorite one. You can perform it before you go to bed—it gives you a restful sleep after a busy day—or before you go to work/school, which will help you be more relaxed and balanced. Or you perform the exercise whenever you need it throughout the day. Once you are used to it, it will take about five minutes to perform. It may take a bit of practice before you get used to it but give it a try and see how you like it.

- Choose your favorite meditation music.
- Sit comfortably.
- Close your eyes and breathe deeply. Let the air fill your lungs completely, and as your lungs get full, breathe in even more air and slowly fill your stomach. Hold your breath for a brief moment and then slowly release it. Repeat two or three times.
- Breathe in to the count of 4, hold to the count of 4 and breathe out to the count of 8. Repeat two or three times.

- Now imagine thick, gnarly roots that come out of the soles of your feet and grow deep into the ground until they reach the center of the Earth.

- At the center of the Earth is a river. Imagine that your roots keep growing until their tips touch the water.

- Breathe in deeply, and as you breathe in, imagine that you collect all of the negative and excess energy from within your body in the center of your core.

- As you breathe out, imagine that this energy is being pushed down your body, through your feet and into the roots. The energy will flow down your roots and into the water, and then it will be washed away by the river.

- Repeat four to five times until all the negative energy is gone.

- Imagine a ball of golden healing energy forming at your roots and moving up into your body, through your body, and out at the top of your head, connecting you with the divine source.

Now you can begin to meditate, connect with your guides, or start your healing practice.

This grounding technique is a wonderful way to end the day. It is very cleansing and rejuvenating.

Notes:

"When you are afraid to face your feelings,
it just means you are apprehensive about being

overwhelmed by emotions that are difficult to feel."

—Matt Kahn

The 7 Chakras

The chakras are energy centers within your body. In the western world, we generally work with the seven main chakras. When I say seven main chakras, I mean the chakras that sit along your spine. There are many more. For example, in the palms of your hands, your fingertips, the soles of your feet, and each of your toes, as well as your knees and elbows. You also have several chakras below your body and above it. But for the purpose of this book, I will focus solely on the commonly known seven main chakras.

Each chakra is located at a specific point along your spine. They are associated with specific body parts and organs, but they are also associated with specific moods, feelings, ailments, and your overall spiritual development.

The word "chakra" is Sanskrit and means "vortex," or "spinning wheel."

Each chakra is associated with one specific color of the rainbow (but also resonates with several similar colors) and one tone on the scale. I find this incredibly interesting and insightful. The seven colors of the rainbow, seven notes on the scale, and seven chakras in the human body. It shows that the energy that vibrates within us also vibrates in everything around us. Everything is connected.

The Root Chakra:

The root chakra is located at the base of your spine, or more precisely at the coccyx, which is the triangular bone in between the vagina or penis and the opening of the anus. This chakra is the earthly foundation of the chakra system. If it is out of balance, you are ungrounded, which means you will feel anxious, nervous, or—similar to me—like a headless chicken. You literally feel as if the ground has been ripped out from under you. You are struggling to find your emotional, and sometimes physical, balance. You get agitated and disoriented. It is very easy for the root chakra to become unbalanced. The sooner you realize that the quicker you can ground yourself.

The root chakra is associated with the colors red, brown, and black. It vibrates to the lower C note. Associated organs are skin, uterus, appendix, and bladder.

The Sacral Chakra:

The sacral chakra is located right below the navel and is ruling the male and female reproductive systems. If this chakra is out of balance, you may have infertility issues, low self-esteem, low sex drive, and money problems, and you may feel pretty worthless. You may feel as if the sky is falling. If the root chakra is out of balance, chances are, the sacral chakra is also affected. If this chakra is in balance, you will feel content with who you are, you will feel balanced, happy, sure of yourself, and have a healthy sex drive. Problems seem like easily solvable challenges.

The sacral chakra is associated with the colors orange, red, and brown, and it vibrates to the D note. Associated organs are skin, gallbladder, pancreas, large intestines, and small intestines.

The Solar Plexus Chakra:

The solar plexus chakra is located at the solar plexus, above the navel and below the heart. It rules your ego. If this chakra is unbalanced, you question your self-worth, your faith in yourself, and your willpower. You may feel as if you are as insignificant as humanly possible. On the other hand, if this chakra is in balance, you have a healthy self-esteem, and you have the courage to do the things that frighten you. You succeed because you know you can.

The solar plexus chakra is associated with the colors yellow and orange, and it vibrates to the E note. Associated organs are skin, liver, stomach, spleen, kidneys, and adrenal glands.

The Heart Chakra:

The heart chakra is located at the physical heart. It is all about love. Love for yourself. Love for others. When this chakra is out of balance, you have trouble giving and receiving love. You tend to shy away from relationships because of past hurts, and even the love of someone else can make you feel hurt. When this chakra is open, you have a spring in your step, and you enjoy life to the fullest. Love is all around and is an amazing feeling.

The heart chakra is associated with the colors pink and green, and it vibrates to the F note. Associated organs are skin, lungs, and heart.

The Throat Chakra:

The throat chakra is located at your throat. It is all about communication. Closely connected to your heart chakra, it is the outlet of your emotions. What the heart wants to express, the throat chakra can put into words.

A throat chakra imbalance is a common issue in women. This stems mostly from their upbringing. They are taught to be silent and sweet and to never speak their mind, at least to some degree. It is very important for women to find their voices. And bringing the throat chakra into balance is a great first step!

When this chakra is out of balance, you tend to have difficulty expressing what you feel or think out of fear of misunderstandings, rejection, or consequences. When this chakra is in balance, you will tell it like it is and won't shy away from expressing how you think or feel, knowing that nothing bad will happen to you when we do.

The throat chakra is associated with the colors blue and green, and it vibrates to the G note. Associated organs are skin, thyroid, parathyroid glands, and thymus gland.

The Third Eye Chakra:

The third eye chakra is located between your eyebrows, at the height of the pituitary gland. This chakra is the chakra of vision. When this chakra is out of balance, you have problems envisioning what you want to achieve. You may feel stuck, not knowing what to do or where to go from where you are. You lack the foresight to determine if a choice is good or bad. Your intuition is failing you. When this chakra is in balance, however, you know exactly what you want and have a sense of how you are going to achieve it.

The third eye chakra is associated with the colors white, purple, and indigo, and it vibrates to the A note. Associated organs are skin, brain, pineal gland, pituitary gland, and hypothalamus.

The Crown Chakra:

The crown chakra is located above your head. It is the center of your balance, both physically and spiritually. It is also your spiritual foundation. If this chakra is out of balance, you may feel light-headed and dreamy, not in the here and now. You may become impatient and annoyed fairly quickly. (The saying "patience is a virtue" comes to my mind as I am writing.) When this chakra is in balance, you have all the patience in the world, you feel content with every aspect of who you are, and you feel grounded in your spirituality and/or religious beliefs.

The crown chakra is associated with the colors indigo, white, and purple, and it vibrates to the H note. Associated organs are skin, brain, pineal gland, pituitary gland, and hypothalamus.

As you have probably noticed, each lower chakra has an upper chakra counterpart. The root chakra is the counterpart of the crown chakra, the sacral chakra is the counterpart of the third eye chakra, and the solar plexus chakra is the counter part of the throat chakra, with the heart chakra being at the center of our being. Everything is connected. As above, so below.

Exercise:

Let's do something fun! Let's determine how well your chakras are spinning. To do that, you will need a pendulum. If you don't have a pendulum and don't want to get one, take a ring, either gold or silver, and hang it on a string that is about twelve inches long.

Stand up straight and hold the pendulum in front of your body. Start with the root chakra. Hold your pendulum at the height of your genitals and wait. For this exercise, the pendulum has to be very still. It will begin to spin, after a brief moment, in the direction your chakras are spinning. By the speed and range of motion, you can determine how open or closed your chakras are. (Take note of each chakra in the list below.)

If the pendulum spins in a rather small circular motion, your chakra is most likely blocked. If your pendulum spins in an extremely wide circular motion that makes it seem almost horizontal, then your chakra is too open.

A healthy range of motion is in between these two extremities. Once you have determined the range of motions of your chakras, you can get a better picture of the issues you are facing at the moment.

In the following chapters, I will show you how you can then bring your chakras back into balance. I would suggest that you reassess your chakras after you've balanced them and then check them again in a month to see which chakra has gone unbalanced once more.

It is not uncommon for chakras to get out of balance rather quickly if you have not yet addressed the root cause. Don't get discouraged if one or more chakras keep getting out of balance. Instead, see it as a guide toward what needs your attention. Emotional healing, just like any other type of growth and transformation means one step forward and two steps back. This is an important process, as it allows you the time to learn what is truly holding you back. Oftentimes, it is something completely different from what you thought.

Root Chakra:

Does it swing? ________________________________

How much? ________________________________

Which direction? ________________________________

Notes:

____
____
____
____
____
____
____
____
____
____

Sacral Chakra:

Does it swing? ____
How much? ____
Which direction? ____

Notes:

Solar Plexus Chakra:

Does it swing? _________________________________

How much? _________________________________

Which direction? _________________________________

Notes:

____

____

____

____

____

____

____

____

____

____

____

____

____

Heart Chakra:

Does it swing? _________________________________

How much? _________________________________

Which direction? _________________________________

Notes:

____

____

____

Throat Chakra:

Does it swing? _______________________________

How much? _________________________________

Which direction? ____________________________

Notes:

Third Eye Chakra:

Does it swing? ____
How much? ____
Which direction? ____

Notes:

____
____
____
____
____
____
____
____
____
____
____
____
____
____

Crown Chakra:

Does it swing? ____
How much? ____
Which direction? ____

Notes:

____
____

My Life-Changing Chakra A-Ha-Moment

You're probably wondering why I'm making such a fuss about the chakras. The reason lies within a very profound experience I had in 2010. This experience was truly eye-opening, and it gave me a whole new view of the power of our own minds and how they can control every aspect of our beings, including the health of our chakra systems.

In my early twenties, I went to get checked to see if I would be able to have children. I had been worried because my menstrual cycles were all over the place, and a couple of years prior, I had needed emergency surgery to remove an ovarian cyst. It left the ovary intact, but the doctors could not guarantee that it would still function. I had an appointment at the local hospital, where two nurses performed an X-ray test called hysterosalpingogram, or HSG. They injected dye into the womb, which then flowed into the fallopian tubes. The dye was then visible on an X-ray. According to their findings, one of my tubes had been blocked, and the other was inconclusive. The final report stated that if I chose to have children, I would need surgery to fix the issue.

This news devastated me. On my way home that day, I was sitting on the train, tears running down my face. I had always wanted to be a mom. That was the only thing I had ever been sure of. Every day that passed after that morning in the hospital, I told myself that I would never have children.

When I first began to study Reiki, about a decade after that fateful day at the hospital, I hardly knew anything about the chakras. What I had heard about them sounded more like spiritual hype than anything else. But then something happened that completely and instantly changed my mind:

During my Level I attunement class, my fellow students and I had to give Reiki to one another and check each other's chakras as part of our training.

So, when it was my turn to be checked, it turned out that my sacral chakra (the one just below the navel) was not spinning at all. It was completely blocked. The pendulum just hung quietly in the air and did not move one bit. My Reiki Master was stunned, as she had never before encountered such a severely blocked chakra. She then worked together with the students to unblock it.

While they were working on me, one of my legs suddenly jolted. This is a common occurrence during Reiki or other energy work. The jolts meant that energy had just catapulted out of my body. Shortly after they finished, I began to feel more balanced, joyful, and enthusiastic. The constant feelings of sadness, despair, and hopelessness began to fade away. And when they checked my sacral chakra once more, it was spinning at a regular pace.

My husband and I had been trying to get pregnant for about four years. After many failed attempts, we had decided to enlist the help of an endocrinologist in order to rule out any physical issues.

When I went to see my new OBGYN, he performed the exact same test I had undergone in the hospital all those years ago. Only, this time the results showed that everything was in perfect working order, without any sign of issues within my fallopian tubes.

When I heard the news, I did not know what to do with that information. So many thoughts and emotions were rushing through me that day. How could that be possible? I had gone to the doctor expecting a confirmation of what I already knew, and yet he told me the exact opposite. For over a decade, I had kept telling myself that I would never have children, and now, all of a sudden, it was supposed to be possible. This did not fit at all into my worldview. I had to adjust my entire mindset.

After the incredible news from my OBGYN and my Reiki attunement, my menstrual cycle began to gradually regulate. Only one year later, I got pregnant, and I am now the mom of an amazing boy.

Let's look at what had happened. First and foremost, I had been forcing my body to believe that it could not carry a child and had therefore blocked my sacral chakra from working as it should. And convincing myself that I would never have children prevented me from questioning the validity of the first test or even considering undergoing a second one to confirm the findings of the first. Even my mom had not been able to change my mind. She had come to visit me the day I had the test and had told me that the body changes every seven years (there's that seven again). She'd said that what was true then may not be true in seven years. But I stubbornly continued to believe that I would never conceive a child.

This whole scenario changed my view about the importance of our chakra systems. It taught me that they are not just a spiritual tool; they are an important physical aspect of our overall health and well-being.

How to Balance the Chakras

Now that we talked in length about the chakras and what we may experience when they are blocked, let's talk about how to unblock them.

Before we begin, I need to stress something: It is imperative that you always begin with your root chakra. The most important rule about working on your chakras is that you must be grounded. If you are not grounded, or if your root chakra is blocked when you work on higher ones, you can create an energy overload in the higher chakras, which can cause anything from headaches to heart flutters (non-medical) to anxiety and panic attacks. When you are grounded, the energy that you are shaking loose can leave your body. If you are not grounded, or your root chakra is not in balance, you can't release this energy. So always begin with your root chakra and work your way up one chakra at a time.

Mudras:

Mudras are special symbolic, or ritual, hand positions in Hinduism and Buddhism. In a regular Tantric ritual, 108 mudras are commonly used. Some mudras involve the whole body, but most of them are performed by only using the hands. You can find mudras in yoga, as well, where they are generally used in combination with certain yogic breathing exercises.

When holding your hands in a certain mudra position, you also chant a specific letter, which comes from an ancient language called "Sanskrit." This chanting will enhance the effect of the mudra by causing a resonance in the body. (I will not go into detail about all of the mudras, as I only use the ones that are associated with the chakras.) Each mudra is accompanied by a specific sound. The pronunciation is quite unique. The "A" is pronounced as "ah," and the "M" is pronounced as "mng." In the beginning, it may seem a bit weird to chant sounds this way, but you will notice how your body begins to vibrate with each chant. After a while, you will also be able to feel how each chakra resonates with its associated sound.

When using the mudras, you should hold your position between five to fifteen minutes for them to be effective. Follow your intuition about the length of each mudra hand position. Each finger position will be held with both hands at the same time unless otherwise specified.

Root Chakra:

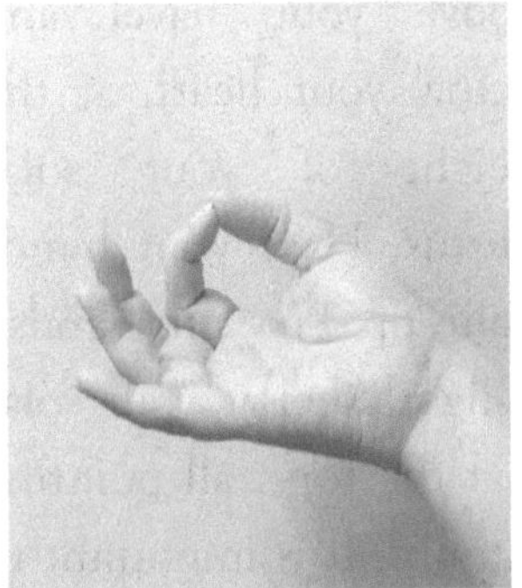

To perform this mudra, the tips of your thumb and index finger should touch, and the other fingers should be relaxed. Focus on your root chakra, which is located at the coccyx, the triangular bone between the genitals and the anus. Chant the sound "LAM." Make it sound like this: "LAAAAAM."

Sacral Chakra:

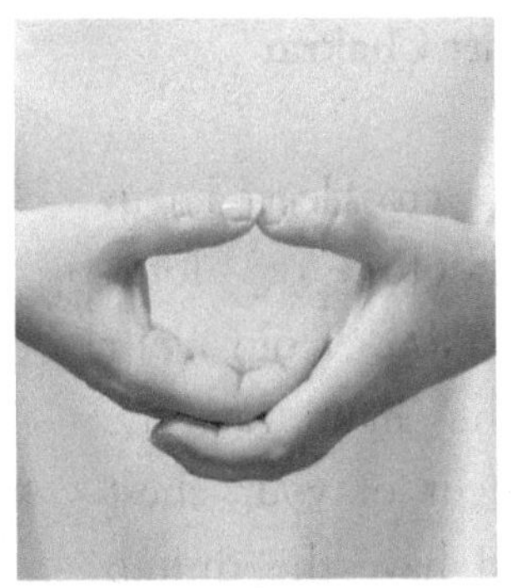

Rest your hands on your legs, your palms up. Now place your right hand over your left and intertwine your fingers. Have your thumbs touch. Focus on your sacral chakra, just below your navel. Chant the sound "VAM." Make it sound like this: "VAAAAAM."

Solar Plexus Chakra:

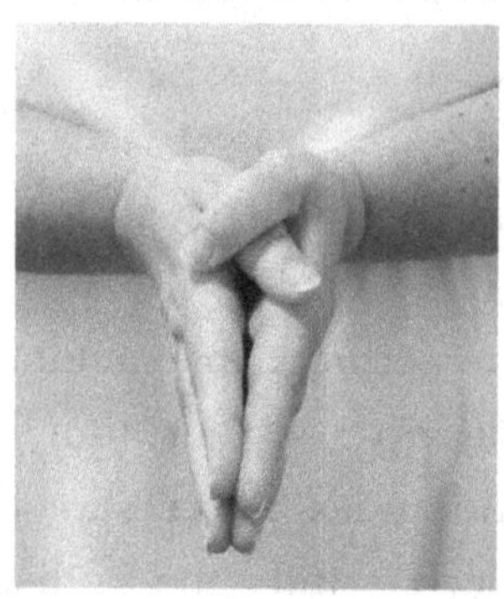

Hold your hands at the height of your stomach, above your navel and below your heart, at the height of your solar plexus. Have your hands palm up. Put your hands in front of your stomach, slightly below your solar plexus. Let the fingers join at the tops, all pointing away from you. Cross the thumbs. It is important to straighten the fingers. Concentrate on the navel chakra, located on the spine, a bit above the level of the navel. Chant the sound "RAM." Make it sound like this: "RAAAAAM."

Heart Chakra:

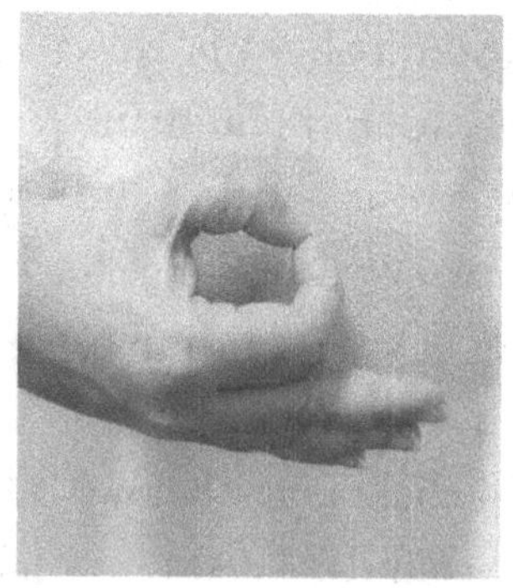

Sit cross-legged, in half-lotus or lotus position. Hold your right hand at the height of your chest and have the thumb and index finger touch to form a circle. The other fingers are slightly stretched outward. Yourleft hand will rest on our knee while the fingers are positioned in the same way. Focus on your heart chakra and chant the sound "YAM." Make it sound like this: "YAAAAAM."

Throat Chakra:

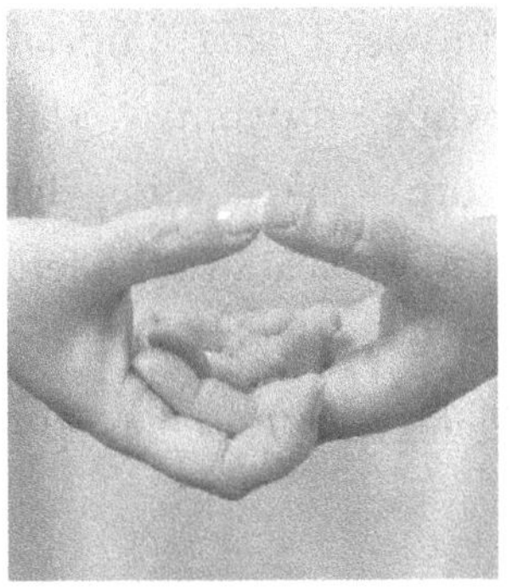

Hold your hands in front of your chest, facing palm up. Cross your fingers inward and have the thumbs touch to form an oval or circle. Focus on your throat and chant the sound "HAM." Make it sound like this: "HUUUUUM."

Third Eye Chakra:

Hold your hands at the height of your solar plexus, just below your chest. Keep your middle fingers straight and touching. The other fingers touch at the knuckles.

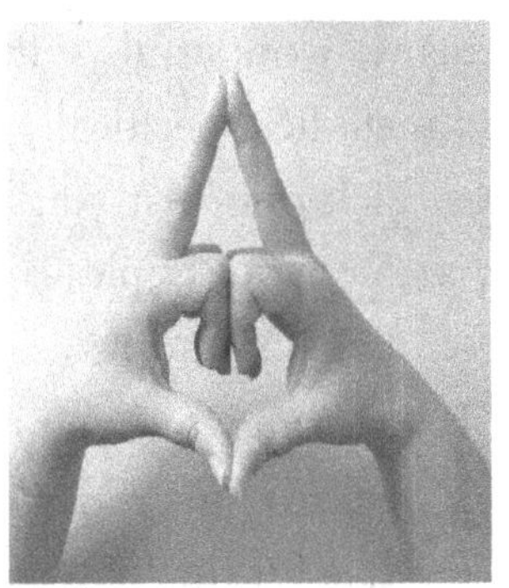

Your thumbs are bent down and touch, as well. Focus on your third eye chakra, slightly above the point between the eyebrows. Chant the sound "OM" or "AUM." Make it sound like this: "AAAAUMMM."

Crown Chakra:

222

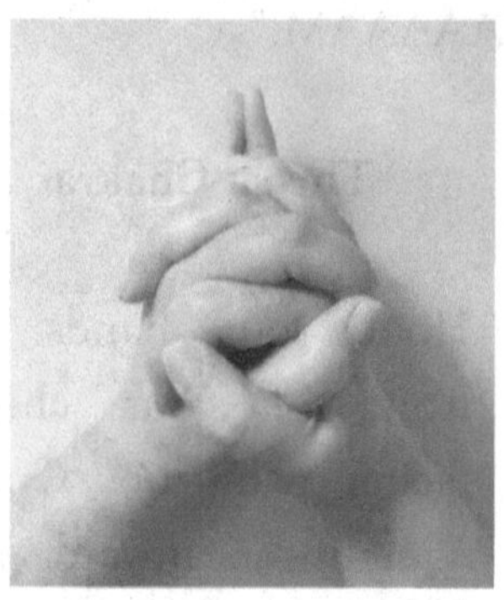

Hold your hands in front of your stomach. All fingers, except the pinkies, cross. The pinkies stay upright while touching. Make sure that the right thumb is above the left

Focus on your crown chakra at the top of your head. Chant the sound "NG." "Make it sound like this: "NNNNNNG."

Music:

As I mentioned in the previous chapter, chakras resonate with music. If you search online, you will find many wonderful spiritual artists who have created melodies specifically designed for each of the chakras. Pick one that you resonate with the most. Below are some examples of how you can make the best use of chakra music:

- Listen to it while you meditate.
- Listen to it and simultaneously use the mudras for the length of each track.
- Listen to it when you go to bed as a bedtime routine.
- Listen specifically to the root chakra music when you feel out of sync, agitated, or anxious.

No matter how you choose to incorporate chakra music into your life, do so consciously. When you listen to the music, focus on it, embrace it, and let it wash over you. You will notice a tingle or vibration in the area of the particular chakra you are working on at that moment.

Singing Bowls:

Singing bowls are usually hand-hammered brass bowls from Nepal or Tibet. They are purchasable one at a time or in a set of up to seven bowls, one for each chakra. During a singing bowl therapy, the therapist uses the clapper on the bowl and then, immediately after, holds the vibrating and humming bowl above the corresponding chakra. The bowl can also be placed directly on the body of the patient as long as he agrees to it and the bowl is not too heavy.

Tunin Forks:

Tuning forks are used in about the same way as singing bowls. Just like singing bowls, you have one tuning fork for each chakra. You can buy them in a set or separately. The desired fork is hit against a hard surface so that it starts humming, and then it is immediately held near the desired area or, in this case, the resonating chakra.

Crystals:

Crystals are a wonderful tool. Even though it is a bit off topic, I will tell you a little story about a bracelet I created for a client a couple years back. She had major issues with PTSD and panic attacks. At this time, I still had my Etsy shop, and she had contacted me to ask me to create an "Ethereal Soul Bracelet" for her, which she was hoping would help her with her issues.

I am a very intuitive person, and so it is only natural for me to use this gift in my jewelry making. When I create an "Ethereal Soul Bracelet," I am connecting with source energy to channel the names of the most suitable crystals for each client. Still to this day, I am in awe over how accurate the crystals that I am receiving from source are.

This bracelet in particular, though, even left me speechless. A couple of weeks after I sent my client her "Ethereal Soul Bracelet," I received a message from her. She said that she had the most profound experience. She received her bracelet just as she was on the verge of a panic attack. She put it on, and the panic attack just vanished.

I don't think that I've ever had a panic attack in my life, so I have no idea what that feels like, but I assume that you cannot just stop a panic attack once it begins. This profound experience my client had truly had me in awe. Of course, I had many other wonderful stories from my clients concerning their "Ethereal Soul Bracelets," but this one was by far the most profound.

If we are open to the healing energy of crystals, they can be an incredible tool. Below, I am listing some of the best crystals for each chakra. Choose the one you feel most drawn to and have it close to you.

Chakra	Crystals
Root Chakra	Fire Agate, Bloodstone, Black Tourmaline, Ruby, Hematite, Tiger's Eye (either red or brown), Garnet
Sacral Chakra	Carnelian, Moonstone, Citrine (the darker version), Copper
Solar Plexus Chakra	Citrine, yellow or orange Calcite, Imperial Topaz, Amber
Heart Chakra	Rose Quartz, Green Aventurine, Green Calcite, Green Jade, Tourmaline, Watermelon Tourmaline
Throat Chakra	Aquamarine, Lapis Lazuli, Sodalite, Turquoise, Celestite
Third Eye Chakra	Clear Quartz, Amethyst, Charoite
Crown Chakra	Amethyst, Diamond, Selenite, Clear Quartz, Howlite

To use crystals to balance your chakras, you can either have a crystal or two in your pockets, wear them as jewelry, or have them close to your body in some other fashion. You can hold one in each hand while meditating, especially while using them with chakra music. You can also place a crystal right in front of you or on your leg while practicing the mudras.

Essential Oils:

If you feel drawn to working with essential oils, you should definitely look into chakra-balancing scents. Here are a few examples of essential oils for your chakras. The list is by no means complete, but it may be a good starting point for you if you feel drawn to it.

Chakra	Essential Oils
Root Chakra	Cloves, Rosemary, Ginger, Cypress, Cedar
Sacral Chakra	Ylang-Ylang, Sandalwood, Myrrh, Bitter Orange, Pepper, Vanilla, Oregano
Solar Plexus Chakra	Lavender, Chamomile, Lemon, Anise, Grapefruit, Fennel (licorice)
Heart Chakra	Rose, Jasmine, Estragon, Cardamom
Throat Chakra	Eucalyptus, Camphor, Peppermint, Roman Chamomile
Third Eye Chakra	Jasmine, Mint, Lemongrass, Violet, Frankincense, Sweet Basil
Crown Chakra	Frankincense, Rosewood

Using essential oils for your chakras is quite simple. Choose the scent you are most drawn to for the day and either place a few drops in your essential oil diffuser jewelry or in your essential oil diffuser at work or at home. The scents will stimulate the appropriate chakra and balance it.

Reiki:

Reiki is a wonderful modality to clear the chakras. If you have been attuned, you will have learned how to clear your own chakras. If you go for a treatment, ask the Reiki practitioner if he or she also works on them. Most of them do. What I find truly fascinating is that you can feel the chakras spinning while you hold your hands over them. During the Reiki treatment, the practitioner will check your chakras. Some use their hands; some use a pendulum. They will check and see if your chakras are open, if they're spinning, how much they're spinning, and which direction they're spinning in.

When it comes to different directions, the opinions vary greatly. I believe that as long as the chakras are open and spinning, it is all good. Ideally, they would all be spinning clockwise. However, there is always a reason why a chakra is spinning counterclockwise. I believe that, in this case, the client is going through a lesson in life or is on the verge of a transformation. I recently had a Reiki student whose entire chakra system spun counterclockwise. Like I said, there is always a reason why chakras spin counterclockwise, and once that reason is resolved, the affected chakra will spin clockwise again. The important thing is that they are spinning.

"It is better to conquer yourself than to win a thousand battles.

Then the victory is yours. It can not be taken from you.

Not by angels or demons, heaven or hell."

—Buddha

Reiki: The Beginning of All Healing

Reiki is a wonderful, holistic healing modality. It is being used in hospitals, especially with cancer patients, as it has proven to decrease the side effects of chemotherapy tremendously and can help patients feel better and experience less pain.

I have been practicing and teaching Reiki since 2010, and I absolutely love it. I have seen some amazing results in myself and in my clients. I would like to share a brief story about when one of my clients and I first met and how Reiki changed her life in only five minutes.

In November of 2017, I was offering a taste of Reiki at a local all-female gym's Christmas bazaar. I had been busy all night, as women were lining up to try Reiki for the first time or to get a quick energy boost for the busy holiday season ahead. Near the end of the evening, three ladies came by my table, and one of them told the other what she knew about Reiki. Well, that woman seemed a bit wary but said, "You know, I have tried everything else, so why not?"

The woman came over and sat down on my table. After I asked her what she would need help with, she said that she had degenerative disk syndrome in her neck and had not been able to move her neck for the past two months. Most days, she had to wear a neck brace because the pain was just too great. That night, she had not worn a neck brace, but she said she was in a lot of pain and was unable to move her neck. I asked her to lie down on the massage table, then began working on her neck. With my hands hovering over her, I scanned the painful area for hotspots, which would be an indication of stuck energy and inflammation. I did not have to search for long. It seemed as if the whole left side of her neck was on fire. Right away, I began to "open a gate" for the energy to flow out of the inflamed area. It felt like a stream of boiling-hot water. I can only imagine how long that woman had been suffering for.

After about five minutes of a constant outpouring of energy, the woman asked me to stop because she felt unbearable heat on her neck. I did as she asked because I sensed that she was startled by what she had just experienced. Under normal circumstances, if we had been in my own healing space, I would have calmed her down and asked her to allow me to release the heat for her. But in this setting and at that moment, I felt it was best to do as she asked. The energy would still continue to release on its own, but at a much slower rate than with my help.

After I helped the lady sit up, I asked her how she felt. She turned her head, looked at me, and said, "I have no pain." I am still getting goose bumps thinking about this moment. The look of disbelief and awe on her face was so wonderful. For the first time in months, she was pain free.

This lady has become one of my regular Reiki clients. She calls me her "Reiki Lady" and has become a true believer in the amazing healing power of Reiki. To this day, she does not quite understand how it works, but that does not matter to her. She hasn't needed a neck brace since then, and after our last session in 2019, she said that for the past six months, she had not had any neck pain at all.

Reiki is very helpful when it comes to chronic pain. And everything else, of course. Sometimes all a person needs is one single session to feel amazing. But most of the time, a sequence of sessions is needed. As you can see from the story above, it took almost three years of quarterly sessions to release the pain from degenerative disc syndrome completely.

With Reiki, there are two different sides. There is the healing side, which many people have heard about and come to cherish, but there is also the spiritual side, which I find has not been getting enough credit in the western world.

Reiki is such a wonderful holistic modality, not just for healing body, mind, and spirit, but also for use in everyday life. Sadly, most people know nothing about it. I hope to spark your interest by telling you a bit more about what it is and what it can do. I believe that everyone should make Reiki a regular part of their health and wellness regime. It should never be a stand-alone treatment option. As an addition, it would enrich your life immensely.

So, what is Reiki? Or rather, what is Reiki not? First and foremost, Reiki is not a Japanese healing modality. Reiki is not even Japanese. Reiki was rediscovered by a Japanese monk named Mikao Usui. It is quite a fascinating story, actually. This Japanese monk was a teacher, a philosopher. One day, his students were raising the question of how Jesus was able to heal. Intrigued by this question, Mikao Usui decided to meditate on this very question in hopes that he would gain insight into that very subject. So he ventured on top of the mountain Kurama, north of Kyoto, and spent ten days fasting and meditating.

On the tenth day, he hit his bare toe on a sharp rock and was bleeding. Instinctively, he placed his hand over the toe, and almost immediately the bleeding stopped. After further meditation, he then received his attunement up on mountain Kurama and was given six Reiki symbols. After his attunement, he went back down the mountain.

After he returned home, his wife complained of a bad toothache. So Mikao Usui did it again. He placed his hand on his wife's cheek, and after a short while, the toothache was gone. This was the beginning of the practices and teachings we know as Usui Reiki.

Receiving visions of symbols sounds pretty "woo-woo," and believe me, if I had not experienced it myself, I would think the same. But when I received my Reiki Master attunement, I also saw symbols I had never seen before. I actually forgot about them for a while, until a book fell into my hands. It was called Reiki Shamanism. I felt drawn to this book, and lo and behold, the symbols I had seen in my mind were in this book. Before I came across Reiki Shamanism, I had never heard about it, but there they were, the symbols I had seen in my mind.

Of course, we can't be sure that the attunement Mikao Usui received was exactly what Jesus did when He healed people. But think about it. Jesus placed His hand over the eyes of a blind woman and made her see. That does not sound much different to me. However, in today's world, the chances are most likely pretty slim that we would ever be able to reach the level of healing Jesus was able to perform, as we have so many energetic distractions from radio waves, environmental pollution, and much more.

So once again, what is Reiki? Reiki is as old as the Earth. Reiki is energy. The name Reiki translates as "life force energy," meaning the energy around us, the energy within us, and the energy that we need in order to exist. Everything is energy. Everything is made from energy. Everything exists because of energy. Without energy, there would be no wind, no rain, no food, no water, no animals, and no us. Energy is what created the planet. It all started with energy. It always starts with energy.

Reiki is a way to bring unbalanced energy back into balance. When you are sick, anxious, or stressed, your energy is out of balance. Unbalanced energy is the beginning of any ailment. With Reiki, you can bring the energy back into balance long before it could potentially transform into physical, mental, or emotional issues.

Let's not forget what Jesus Christ foretold:
"I tell you the truth, anyone who has faith in me will do what I do, what I have been doing. He will do even greater things than these."
(John 14:12) New International Version

Reiki Attunements in a Nutshell

Just in case I sparked your interest about Reiki and you are now wondering how the attunement process works, I will give you some insight. I became a Reiki Master in 2010, and I am so glad I did, as it changed my life in so many ways. Reiki is a wonderful first step in your spiritual path. You see, the healing part of Reiki is just a side effect; a very positive one, but just a side effect. I know that I mentioned this before, but I find it to be so important that I wanted to mention it again.

So, let me talk a bit about what happens before or around the time you decide to get attuned to Reiki. Most people stumble upon Reiki through their search for an alternative healing method. Some will only look for treatments. Others may feel drawn to learning more and maybe even become practitioners themselves. The thing is that you don't find Reiki; Reiki finds you.

I would like to show you, with the support of a few drawings created by my talented friend Janice, how your world-view changes with each Reiki attunement.

Look at this walnut shell. This is your life when you first hear about Reiki. Inside this nutshell is your whole life, everything you know, everything you have been taught, and everything you believe in.

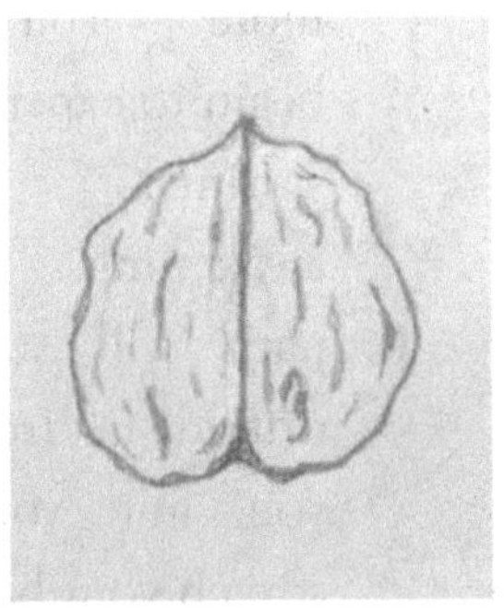

As you can see, the tip of the nutshell is just ever so slightly cracked open. A tiny crack. This symbolizes your view of the world and that tiny glimpse that you received from things outside your world. You are intrigued, and at that point Reiki will find you.

Then, when you receive your first attunement, something incredible happens:

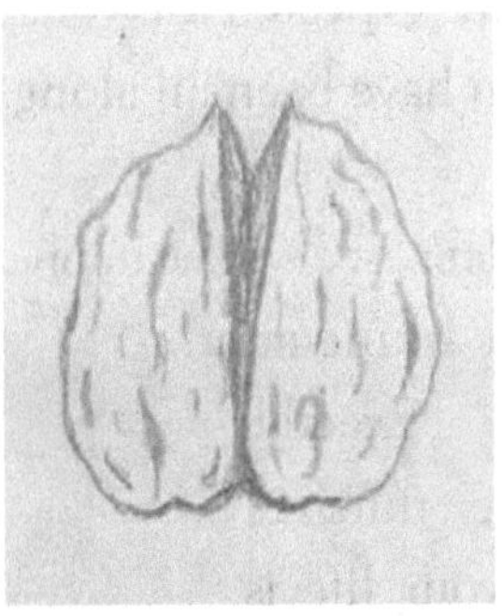

The first attunement opens your world up a little bit more. You will learn to work with the energies around you. You will learn how to work with your spirit guides and how to help heople by giving them Reiki treatments. And you will learn how working with Reiki for yourself will help you to open up spiritually.

In the second attunement, this happens:

The nutshell that is your life will open up even

more. You will begin to experience spiritual awakenings. Your path will start to unfold in front of you, and you will stretch your belief in yourself to your limits, only to realize that there are no limits to what you can

accomplish. You are beginning to question things you have learned, things that used to define you before you were introduced to Reiki, and things your family expected of you. You start to see the person you have been all along.

Now let's see what happens when you receive the Master attunement:

Yep! Exactly! Poof! The nutshell that was your life is gone. You receive the full spectrum of energy. This is why I highly recommend

you wait to do your master/teacher training until you are ready. It can be very overwhelming when you receive access to the endless source of energy.

I often see practitioners or schools who offer all three Reiki levels in one weekend. I personally find this extremely irresponsible. But of course, every person is different.

I love teaching Reiki and passing on my knowledge. For me, it is very important to teach my students everything I know and everything I have learned, and I also encourage them to find their own truths. They may see Reiki and the energies in a completely different light than I did. And that is perfectly all right. We all are here for a very specific reason. We all have a job to do, and as a teacher I am merely giving my students a nudge in the right direction. Where their life then leads them is up to my students and their destiny. I feel humbled by each student who chose me to be their teacher. And I do hope that many other teachers feel the same way about their students.

Reiki is an incredible first step in your spiritual path. You will learn so much just in the first attunement class. You will be opened up to receiving the universal life force energy, and you will learn how to properly use it. You will learn how to use it for your own good and for the good of others. This could be the steppingstone to an amazing spiritual life.

Now, by spiritual life, I don't mean that you will now constantly feel the need to meditate or take every yoga class in town. You will still lead a life just like you had, but you will start to notice things about yourself and others. Things that you might not have noticed before. And the beauty is that you won't be alone on your journey for long. Like-minded people will be drawn to your higher energy. You will run into a lot of people who have the same path or same interests. And you will teach each other. Your path will begin to reveal itself to you.

You don't have to be a Master to be successful in your spiritual path. Many people are happy just to have the first degree. Others will feel drawn to receiving all three attunements as soon as possible. There is really no right or wrong way. Whatever you feel is the right way for you generally is. Now, this does not mean that it may not change some-where down the road, but always trust that the current path will lead you to the next intersection of your life. There is no right or wrong way. Whichever path you choose is the right one for you at that very moment. And later, when you feel that this path is no longer in your best interest, you simply choose another one. Just by deciding that you want to do something else, you are already set onto the path to change.

"In the process of letting go

you will lose many things from the past,

but you will find yourself."

–Deepak Chopra

Nightmares Versus Transformational Dreams

Many trauma survivors suffer from horrible nightmares. This is, unfortunately, a normal phenomenon. Nightmares symbolize the feelings you try to suppress. To get rid of the nightmares, you have to diligently work on releasing your trauma. Once you are at a point where you feel at least neutral, if not at peace with what happened, the nightmares will disappear. Everything your body and mind do is a reflection of what needs your attention. During the day, you can be pretty good at suppressing your trauma, but at night, when your conscious mind is out of commission, your subconscious mind can make itself known, and it is usually in the form of nightmares.

But not all nightmares are actual nightmares. Sometimes your subconscious mind is trying to send you messages through your dreams. And in this chapter, I want to talk about those dreams. I call those types of dreams transformational dreams. Transformational dreams may seem like nightmares simply because you are not just observing a situation; you take an active part in it.

There is one dream in particular that I would like to mention here, as it is a very common dream of sexual abuse survivors. It is not uncommon for a sexual assault or rape survivor to dream about having sex with his or her abuser. But in the dream, the roles are reversed. The abuser is the victim, on the bottom, and the victim is on top, in control. This dream can cause a turmoil of emotions in the trauma survivor. He or she might ask the question, "What is wrong with me?"

Let me make something very clear: There is absolutely nothing wrong with you if you have had this dream. The sexual act, in its basic form, is a "dance" of the physical aspect of the soul. The merging of two bodies to become one and move in unison. At least, that's how it should be. But when it comes to abuse, this is not the case. In the case of abuse, it is all about dominance, conquest, and power. So, when you are dreaming of reversed roles, your subconscious mind is trying to show you that you can get your power back. The power you deemed lost due to the assault. Showing you a dream where you are in the power role simply means that you are ready to take your power back. And it has absolutely nothing to do with the sexual act. The sexual act in the dream stands as a metaphor, as an explanatory image.

Here is another example of a transformational dream that some may have experienced. This one is about a clown. And in this dream, you may kill the clown, and it just comes back to life over and over again. Spooky, right? But the message this dream sends is not spooky at all; it's rather quite insightful. In this dream, you are fighting with your limiting beliefs. Deep down, you believe that you are a joke and that no one takes you seriously, which is symbolized by the clown, and yet you try to prove everybody, including yourself, wrong. This is portrayed by you killing the clown. What this shows you is that you have to believe in yourself before you can see change. The outside world is a mirror to what is happening within yourself. So, in order to stop feeling like a joke, you have to heal what makes you believe you are just that. You have to work on our self-love and self-esteem.

I find dream interpretation truly fascinating. Our dreams can reveal so much to us that can help us in our healing journey. My rule of thumb is that if you can remember a dream in detail, then you are supposed to.

If you are prone to vivid dreams, I would encourage you to create a dream journal. Have a journal beside your bed, and whenever you wake up from a dream, write it down in as much detail as possible. Even though the dream may have been terrifying, understand that there is always a reason why you dream and especially why you remember a dream. The following day, when you are ready, read what you wrote about your dream. Then try and recall it. View it like a movie. Be an observer and see if you can understand what the dream is trying to tell you. Think about feelings, sensations, smells, colors, your surroundings etc. When it comes to dream interpretation, think outside the box.

What have you noticed about a particular dream you had?

____

____

____

____

____

____

____

____

____

____

____

____

____

____

____

____

Trauma and Your Hair

Here is an approach to trauma healing and life transformation that is completely outside the box. Your hair. What do you really know about your hair? How does it make you feel to have it long or short? How do you feel after you've dared to cut your long mane off for a pixie cut? Does it feel liberating? Daring? Sexy? Scary?

In many cultures, hair is seen as something sacred, an extension of us. This is especially the case in Native American tribes and in Asia. In those cultures, hair only gets cut in extremely specific circumstances. Native tribes believe that hair holds the energy of the past. Therefore, they cut their hair only after experiencing significant loss, trauma, death of a close family member, or other significant life-changing events. The cut strands are then treated with the utmost respect and are burned, buried, or otherwise preserved.

I am sure you have heard that after a breakup or divorce, women often change their hair. For some, it almost feels like a need. Those women feel the difference of a new haircut. Cutting off the past few years of a relationship that has broken apart is like finding closure, moving on, leaving it all behind. It does make sense, doesn't it?

Hair holds both positive and negative energy. It is an extension of your mind, holding your thoughts, emotions, stress, hopes, and fears. Cutting your hair is healthy, not just for your hair, but for your overall health and well-being.

Lately, have you been feeling drawn to cut your hair but have not dared to do it out of fear of whether you will like it, or rather whether the world will like it? Or is it your ego trying to hold on to the negative energy that needs to be released in order for you to move on? Think about it.

How do we know how many years of energy we are carrying around with us? You see, six inches is approximately what hair grows in a year, so every six inches of hair represents one year and holds the energy of that year. If you have long hair, measure it and see how long it is. Then divide it into six-inch increments and see how many years of energy you are holding on to.

Just recently, I cut my long hair off, and I now have a nice, short haircut. This is not the first time I have done this. I am one of the lucky ones, as my hair grows pretty quickly. I've had hair down to my waist twice now in the past ten years, and both times I cut it really short once I reached that length.

I've recently cut off the past two and a half years of my life, when I went through some pretty rough times. It was so liberating, cutting off that energy and being rid of it for good. I had also felt that with my long hair, I was hiding. And if you read the chapter "Another Paper Cut Story," you will remember that I did everything to make myself invisible. Yet at some point, I was ready to be seen again, and I felt it was time for a drastic change. So I cut off my hair and dyed it blond. It felt awesome!

Will you dare to cut your hair and release the energy you are holding on to?

Notes:

____

____

____

____

____

____

____

____

____

____

____

____

____

Trauma and Allergies

Allergies are an interesting phenomenon. We know allergies to be a hypersensitivity of the body to various food items, fur, pollen, and other substances. But did you know that allergies can also be caused by trauma? And not just that. We can also be made to believe that we have allergies and then actually show allergic reactions. I have seen this phenomenon in several people.

One of my friend's mother used to be a clean freak. She scrubbed everything and made sure her children constantly washed their hands and wore clean clothes. This environment made it incredibly stressful for my friend, and she became allergic to different cleaning products, various foods, and many other things. Well, when the time came for her to go to college and she moved out, within six months most of her allergies disappeared.

Another friend of mine told me that his mother was very controlling and manipulative. She used whatever mental means necessary to control her children. When she made dinner and one of them did not like something or felt sick after eating it, she was certain that her child had had an allergic reaction to one of the ingredients used in that meal. So my friend was told that he was allergic to onions, eggs, fish, pets, and all sorts of other things from a young age on. For him, it was the same story. Once he distanced himself from his family and moved away, the allergies disappeared.

When your mind and body are conditioned to believe what you are told is true, you will take that belief as truth. You will internalize it, and your body and mind will behave as if it were real.

If your body can be made to believe it has allergies, how might your body react when deep trauma is a part of the problem?

I met a woman once who was allergic to almost anything under the sun. She could not drink dairy or eat eggs, gluten, or even certain fruits and vegetables. She had to live off a very controlled and narrow diet. The interesting thing was that she never used to have allergies. They just appeared one day...after she had miscarried her twin girls. She was never able to overcome the grief she felt. She blamed herself, or rather her body, for not being able to carry children. This made her reject her own body. The allergies were a result of that rejection—

rejection of nourishing herself to punish herself for what had happened.

I am not saying that allergies are not real. On the contrary. I myself am allergic to nickel and to fresh pineapple, which really upsets me because I love fresh pineapple. However, the stories above show that it is possible for trauma to create allergic reactions when there are no true allergies present.

Notes:

The Healing Vibes of Music

I love music, and I bet you do, too. Music can be a great way to release that stressful day at work or the last nerve-racking family reunion.

When my clients feel stressed or overwhelmed in their everyday lives, I always encourage them to dance it out. Dancing is the one thing that all cultures share. Dancing can be a ritual, a rite of passage, and a joyful experience. Dancing and joy go hand in hand. So it is safe to say that when we are dancing and truly immerse ourselves in the rhythm, we cannot be stressed or depressed.

Music, especially lyrics, can have an amazing effect on us. Why don't you create a few music files on your device of choice for different occasions? How about a rhythmic party mix that you can dance to during the times when you can't seem to shake off excess energy? How about a mix of meditative or relaxing music for your salt bath or meditation? I would also recommend a folder of inspirational songs that give you the courage to step out of your comfort zone and grow.

I love music, and I love dancing to some of the early techno beads from the 90s, like KLF, Cappella, 2 Unlimited, etc.

The beat just vibrates through and through. And the more you allow the beat to penetrate your system, the better you will feel after you've danced all of the excess energy out of your body.

Here is how it works: When you are feeling stressed, you hold on to that energy. You block your lower chakras and feel unbalanced, edgy, emotional, upset, and maybe even anxious. The rhythm of the music you resonate with will flow through your body, and the vibration will loosen that pent-up energy. When you dance, you are creating more balance within your body because dancing also creates vibration within yourself. This vibration will raise your energy and release the negative or excess energy that has been accumulating in your system.

I find the concept of energy and vibrations truly fascinating. Don't you? In the lines below, write down your experience of a dance-out you had after a rough day or week:

____

____

____

____

____

____

____

____

____

____

Which songs inspire you or make you feel like you could conquer the world? For me, it is "Fight Song" by Rachel Platten and "Road Less Traveled" by Lauren Alaina.

Remember that we are all spiritual beings having human experiences. The soul knows of all the amazing spiritual possibilities, but it is not the soul's job to make the ego understand. (I will dive deeper into the purpose of the soul in the two following books of this series 'How to Unbecome Who You Were Taught To Be' and 'How To Become Your True Self')

Respect Your Journey

Being on your life's journey, it is important to understand that you are always exactly where you are supposed to be, even if you feel that you took a wrong turn at some point, because that wrong turn shows you what is not working. There is never a wrong decision. Each decision you make either advances you or teaches you a lesson. Both are imperative to your journey and growth! Always keep that in mind. The path itself is not important, but the knowledge you gained is. If everything always went smoothly, you would not learn anything. Only through hurdles, downfalls, and roadblocks do you learn and advance. If everything just fell into your lap, you would never evolve. To truly appreciate what you have and who you are, you have to first live without it. Knowing that you achieved everything you have by yourself is an incredibly empowering feeling!

Never doubt your path! If it does not feel right, change direction. But never resent any part of your path. Everything you went through made you the person you are today and will shape who you will become in the future.

For years, I kept asking myself why I had to endure sexual assault and rape. Now I know that it was part of my journey to my life's purpose. Only by experiencing it myself and overcoming the emotional trauma caused by it am I truly able to understand how other people feel inside and give them a hand on their way back to themselves.

No experience is ever a waste of time! You just have to connect the dots to understand its purpose.

Be Kind to Yourself:

Be kind to yourself. Healing from trauma is a journey. You can take one step forward only to be thrown three steps back. Be patient with yourself. As long as you choose to never give up, to move forward no matter how many setbacks you have to experience, you are on the right track.

Be kind to yourself. Trauma healing is not just about letting go of the past and getting your life back together. It is also about self-love and being stronger than you thought you could ever be. Yet, at the same time, it is about being compassionate toward yourself and others.

Be kind to yourself. If you are not ready to forgive the person who caused you pain, don't punish yourself. Accept where you are at this point. Love yourself unconditionally, and you will see that by loving yourself no matter what, you will reach your goals much faster.

Be kind to yourself. As a trauma survivor, you already feel worthless, undeserving of love and compassion. You often see the fault in yourself, especially for the sexual assault or domestic abuse you experienced. So you punish yourself because you feel you deserve to be punished. You punish yourself for wanting to let the past go, and you punish yourself for not getting over it. There is always one reason or another for you to punish yourself. Please don't.

Be kind to yourself. Especially when you feel undeserving of love. Especially when you believe that it was your fault. Always be kind to yourself. Be kind to yourself and give yourself all the time you need to heal.

Be Kind to yourself, and always remember:

TRAUMA IS NOT
A LIFE SENTENCE

YOU HAVE
THE POWER TO HEAL

How Can I Help?

This chapter is for anyone who knows someone who has been through a traumatic incident. This is for all of the parents, sisters, brothers, aunts, uncles, grandparents, friends, and best friends who don't know how to approach and handle learning about the story of another person's abuse.

For many, trauma is a taboo subject. They don't want to talk about it, they don't want to hear about it, and they don't want to know about it. Most trauma survivors see this behavior or attitude as an attack or a dismissal of their story, their needs, and themselves. It just makes them feel even more alone than they already believe they are.

Trauma is something that happens to other people, not to our children, our friends, and loved ones. Most people cannot fathom that their loved one had to experience something so vile and horrific. And they don't know how to handle their own feelings toward it.

I have talked to many trauma survivors and asked them what they wish had happened after they were traumatized. And they all said, "I wish I had someone to talk to. I wish I had someone who believed in me and just listened. I wish I had someone who would have just given me a hug and told me, 'I've got you! It is going to be okay.'"

Here is what most of the trauma survivors said they were told when they tried to reach out:

- Can't you just let it go?
- Don't you think it is time you got over it?
- This happens to a lot of people.
- This happened to me, too. Do you see me whine about it?
- I don't believe you.

When you think about those words, they all sound very harsh, don't they? And yet they all come from the same source: FEAR and PAIN. Fear of not being the right person to talk to, fear of making it worse, fear of not being able to handle the images that pop into the mind, fear of being triggered, and fear of messing it up. Pain from memories and the lack of support. Pain for a child, friend, or family member. Guilt and shame for not being there to help prevent it. Guilt and shame for not seeing the signs.

But here is the thing: If your friend or family member reached out to you, that means that she believes you are the right person to confide in. She trusts you; she believes in you. For the most part, she is not looking for advice; she is just looking for someone to talk to. Being able to talk about trauma can be so healing in itself. Not having to keep it inside any longer; letting it out. Putting it into words can bring so much healing, clarity, and even freedom.

What I would implore you to do is shift your focus from your own emotions and focus all of your attention on the person who asked for help. You can focus on yourself after you've helped your child, family member, or friend. Your feelings are just as valuable—there is no doubt about it—but right in that moment, you are needed. You can do this!

So, take a deep breath, center yourself, and then look at him or her and ask, "What do you need?" or "How can I help?" I guarantee you, this person will tell you what she needs. Because she knows. It may begin with the need to just be believed or feel heard, or it may just be a hug. You both will gradually build up rapport, and that will empower you both.

I see so many parents who punish themselves because they vowed to never let this happen to their child and yet it did. Dear parents, please understand, this was not your fault. There was nothing you could have done. There is no need to feel guilty for the rest of your life. You can still help your child! Be there for her now. Help her heal by simply asking what she needs and support her on her healing journey. This is the greatest gift you can give her and yourself. It will help you both heal and strengthen your bond. And what's more, you show your child how she can support her own children someday. You will empower her in more ways than one. And when she is old, she will remember, not her trauma, but how you were there for her after it happened.

Holding on to trauma is a prison that we create within ourselves because we have lost our foundation, we have lost our faith in people, and we have lost our self-worth. You, dear parents, can help your child release himself or herself from that prison, rebuild his or her foundation, and rediscover his or her self-worth. But this is only possible through love, compassion, and patience. Just like grief, trauma healing will take as long as it takes, but having someone she loves to be there for her can help her immensely.

If you are a parent and would love to help your child but don't know how or where to start, please reach out. Together, we can find a way to help you heal and support your child.

"Incredible change happens in your life when you decide

to take control of what you do have power over

instead of craving control over what you don't."

–Steve Maraboli

Fascinating Trauma Healing Modalities

When it comes to trauma healing, there is no one-size-fits-all approach. You are an individual who has an individual story, an individual mindset, and individual needs. A modality that works for one person may be completely wrong for another. It all depends on your readiness, the stage of healing you are in, and what you are open to exploring.

Science has finally caught up with what holistic practitioners have known for many years: Trauma affects the whole body. Many new, or rather lately-brought-to-light, healing techniques and modalities have gained interest and popularity.

I am so excited to have some wonderful experts talk about their trauma healing modalities and share some inspirational stories with you. These modalities are very interesting ones that can help you as a stand-alone modality or as an addition to an already-existing treatment plan.

GRAHAM NICHOLLS is an expert in human emotional and behavioral psychotherapy as well as a leader in the areas of strategic life coaching, NLP, EFT/TFT, mindfulness, CBT, and multi-discipline  psychotherapy. Through his teaching, he helps people to fulfill their dreams of joining the incredible helping industry as helping/psychotherapy practitioners, and he also assists clients from around the world to achieve their life's goals, dreams, and ambitions. Graham will introduce you to the fascinating world of EFT and talk about how it can help you release trauma.

 **MELISSA TAR** is a therapeutic recreational therapist, traumatic incident reduction (TIR) facilitator, and published author. In her business, Embrace Rec, she helps her clients embrace life to the fullest with fun activities and

challenging tasks. Her main focus is children and adolescents.

Being a victim of child abuse herself, she did not have to look far for her passion and purpose. Melissa is the author of the children's book The Brave Little Brown Bear, which is a beautifully written story about a little bear who has to face his fears and learn valuable lessons in the process.

DEVANNI PETERS is a holistic health coach, with focus on Ayurvedic natural medicine, as well as a yoga instructor. She was one of sixteen siblings in a Mennonite family. As a young child, she began to observe her family and questioned routines that did not make sense to her. She found her way into spirituality and fell in love with the amazing practice of yoga. In December 2020 she published her first book, From Mennonite to Yogi. Devanni will introduce you to the wonderful practice of yoga and show you how it can help you heal from trauma.

SANDRA COOZE, which is me, will be talking about T.I.R. (traumatic incident reduction), trauma release and self-empowerment coaching, crystals, and Reiki. There are many more amazing modalities out there that can support you  in your trauma healing journey. For example, gestalt therapy, somatic experiencing, acupuncture, sound therapy, eye movement desensitization, muscle testing, etc. I am really hoping that the following chapters will inspire you to look for an out-of-the-box trauma healing approach.

EFT & TFT The Tapping Journey

by Graham Nicholls

Have you ever been so amazed by something that you had to check it over and over to make sure that what you saw, heard, or felt was real? This is the effect that tapping had on me. Whether you call it TFT (thought field therapy), EFT (emotional freedom techniques), or any of the other names it has taken on, tapping is quickly becoming one of the most used complementary therapies.

Let's start at the beginning of the journey, shall we? Not the beginning of my journey, but the beginning of the tapping journey. A brief history, if you will. Dr. Roger Callahan is the originator of tapping, choosing to tap on various points on the body rather than stick needles in, as is done in acupuncture. He discovered that using certain points on the body's meridian (or energy) systems could have an effect on freeing them from blockages.

He and his wife spent many years experimenting with differing ways of tapping and different algorithms (or tapping sequences) to clear various emotional issues. What they discovered was that it wasn't just emotional issues that they could help with; pain and trauma were also positively affected by the simple act of tapping.

Dr. Callahan called this new technology "thought field therapy," or TFT. At the most basic of levels, he would have people rate their issues on a scale of one to ten, where one means no issue and ten means it is the worst it has ever been. He would then have them tap on certain points of the body, in a certain order, and then have them re-rate the issue and repeat the process. The results were astounding, showing that around 80 percent of people showed a positive outcome that lasted.

As the Callahans developed this further, they began to teach it to others so that the healing powers of this amazing modality could be spread far and wide. One of their students took on their work and developed it into something he would call EFT, or emotional freedom techniques. That student was Gary Craig, the man now recognized as the creator of the tapping revolution.

Most people have heard of EFT rather than TFT because Gary Craig did two main things: He made the process simpler so that you don't have to remember many different sequences, and he took the whole thing into the mainstream. Tapping grew from there, and it continues to grow, to this day, as one of the most powerful helping therapies in the world.

Gary Craig said, "The cause of all negative emotion is a disruption in the body's energy system." Since Gary Craig started the EFT revolution, it has been taken on and developed into many other forms by various people. It has been changed, modified, and generally messed about with, to the point where there are simply too many "versions" of it to remember. Yet, at the heart of all of this, what we are really talking about here is gently tapping on a few different points on your body, which has a massive impact on your life.

So, where does my journey into the world of tapping begin? Well, a few years ago, I started looking into alternative therapies for reducing chronic pain levels. My wife has a severe neck and spinal injury due to a car crash many years ago, and despite taking many tablets each day, she still has consistent pain. I knew that there had to be something out there that could help but didn't involve more medication, and from my searching I found Dr Callahan's work. I was so intrigued that I didn't just help my wife with it; I used it for myself and started to dig deeper into the fascinating world of tapping. I discovered the work of Gary Craig. I watched, listened, and read everything I could, and eventually I attended a couple of training courses to become a practitioner/master practitioner. My love affair with tapping was in full flow.

As a coach, I helped clients with it, and then, finally, I started to teach it online so that many more people could benefit from its amazing properties. I marvel at the stories people tell me about how it has changed their lives or the lives of the people they have gone on to help. I've heard people tell me how they help underprivileged children to cope with life, and I've heard of people who have been released from the consequences of their past traumatic experiences. Truly amazing!

Dr. Wayne Dyer said, "Put away your skepticism, this really works. I've had great results with tapping in my own life."

Where would this journey be if I didn't allow you to understand the benefit for yourself, if I didn't give you a taste of the incredible benefits this could have in your life or the lives of those you love and care about? So let's take you on a tapping journey around your body so that you can see, hear, and feel what all this "tapping" is about.

First off, here's the points we are going to tap on throughout this journey;

- **The Karate Chop Point:** Also known as the side of the hand. On the outside of your hand, in between the knuckle of your little finger and your wrist, where any karate sensei would tell you to chop a block of wood in half. This is your starting point, and you are going to tap there while saying a specific phrase three times. (Don't worry, I'll get to the phrase after covering all of the tapping points.)

- **Top of the Head:** Some may call this the crown chakra. This isn't the crown of your head, though; it is closer to your hairline than that. You'll find this about halfway in between your crown and hairline. It's worth pointing out that some of these points might be a little sensitive. Others, though, you may not be able to feel at all. Don't worry about this. Just get in the general area for now.

- **Corner of the Eyebrow:** This is the inside point of the eyebrow, nearest to the nose. It doesn't matter if it is on your left- or right-hand side. Use your dominant hand and see which side feels more comfortable to reach.

- **Outside of the Eye:** This is on the very outside of the eye socket—make sure you are feeling in the bony part of the eye socket—where the oval shape of the eye meets its edge. Warning: Be careful here, as missing and tapping on the eyeball is going to hurt!

- **Under the Eye:** Next, shift to the middle of the bottom of the eye socket, again making certain to find the bony part right underneath where your pupil would be if you were staring straight forward.

- **Collarbone:** Follow your collarbone (either side) toward the center, and eventually you will feel a dip, a small U shape, where each side meets. The tapping spot is on the edge of that U shape, where the collarbone ends. You can tap on either side, or on both at once if you choose.

- **Underarm:** Place your hand right under your armpit and go two-hand widths down the side of your torso to find this spot. For ladies, it is roughly where your bra strap wraps around you.
- **Fingernails:** Take each finger, in turn, from the little one to the ring finger to the middle finger to the forefinger and, finally, to the thumb. The place you are looking for on each finger is at the bottom of the fingernail, at the bottom of that U shape. On each side, you will find the tapping points.
- **Return to the Karate Chop Point:** Repeating the phrasing three times.

You now know all of the tapping points. It might take you a while to find them each time and remember their order, as that only comes with practice.

"Wait a minute, Graham. What's all this about a phrase?" I hear you shout. I'm glad you asked! With the EFT version of tapping, a phrase is repeated throughout the tapping process, out loud if possible, or just to yourself if you prefer. You construct a "long" phrase for tapping on the Karate Chop Point, then shorten it for the rest of the points, and it relates directly to the issue you want to resolve. The best way I can explain this is through an example:

Imagine, for a moment, that I have a client named Sarah who has come to me, and Sarah is struggling with being stressed. Her stress is causing her all sorts of issues, from lack of sleep and health complications to mood swings and family issues. She wants and needs to feel less stress, and she has turned to tapping for some assistance.

The standard phrase we use reads like this: "Even though I have felt (insert issue here), I completely love and accept myself."

So, in Sarah's case, it would be: "Even though I have felt stressed, I completely love and accept myself."

Note the use of past tense in the phrasing—"I have felt stressed"—meaning it is in the past. I cannot overemphasize this part enough, as language plays such a huge part in how you feel. Using past tense language in this way adds to the benefits the tapping will give and therefore makes a vital ingredient in the recipe.

Sarah and I now have the long phrase that she will repeat three times while tapping on the Karate Chop Point at the start and end of the process. For the rest of the tapping points, we are going to tap on them around seven to ten times (no need to count; just approximate) while saying a shorter phrase once on each point. That shorter phrase, in Sarah's case, will be: "I've felt stressed." Again, note the use of past tense even in this shorter version of the phrase.

We are now ready to begin tapping. As a practitioner, I tap on myself at the same time Sarah taps on herself so that she can follow me, as this is all new to her. We start with the Karate Chop Point and repeat the full phrase three times while tapping, then move on to each individual point while saying the shorter phrase. Finally, we return to the Karate Chop Point and repeat the long phrase three times again.

This is one cycle of the process, and it can be repeated as many times as required. Simple, right? It's important to remember that you can't do any harm with this (unless you tap particularly hard and whack yourself in the eye; don't do that!), so it is repeatable for just about any issue. However—and this is an important however—tapping does not have to only be used for resolving emotional and physical issues! The process is every bit adept at helping you to feel good, to relax, to increase energy, and to improve your immune system. Many people only see it as a solution to a particular problem, but like many problems, prevention is better than solution.

I highly recommend finding just ten minutes a day to go through the tapping routine with positive intent. You can find an area to focus on or select a different area each day. It really doesn't matter. Imagine, for a moment, having seven different areas of your life that you want more positive results in and then focus on each of them one day per week. Here's an example of what a week might look like:

Monday: greater energy

Tuesday: increased joy

Wednesday: fulfilled love

Thursday: immune strength

Friday: wonderful health

Saturday: freedom of spirit

Sunday: inner peace

If you worked on those throughout each week, how much would your life improve? I'll let you think about that while I talk you through the simple change of the phrasing. The longer phrase looks like this: "Now that I have (insert positive intent here), I completely love and accept myself." And the shorter phrase is simply: "I have (insert positive intent here)."

So, there you have it. You and I have come to the end of this part of the tapping journey, but it is my sincere hope that it is just the start of your tapping journey. It is a journey that can take you to places you have never imagined, an inner journey to a much better life. Enjoy it!

If you would like to know more about tapping or any of the other helping areas I teach, come and find me at The Priority Academy at www.theprioritvacademy.com.

Recreational Therapy

by Melissa Tar

My childhood memories are vague. This is something that I am thankful for, as the memories I experienced were not typical, or at least I pray that other children didn't have to endure the same turmoil. My parents were rebellious youth, wanting to pave their own paths, without having any true comprehension of the consequences of their actions. Young love produced two children to parents barely old enough to care for themselves, and it was during a time when child protection laws were scarce. My father was a damaged man, lacking judgment or a conscience, and dished out his anger willfully. Their marriage ended. However, his access to us children was without concern or bias.

The curious nature of trauma is that it's a cycle that continues within the family unit, wielding its anger and pain for generations, and it is often blanketed by shame. My father was a young man growing up in a family rippled with secrets that were perpetuated by the precarious ventures of my grandfather. His abuse led to unmanaged anger and fueled rage. I became the innocent victim of sexual and psychological abuse. To this day, I don't know how I found my resiliency, but I decided to break the cycle.

Having survived my trauma, I stand as an example for others grappling with seemingly insurmountable pain. When the opportunity presented itself for me to contribute to this book, I was overwhelmed with both excitement and angst. I was finally going to share my story, including the how and why behind my company, where I work as a recreation therapist and traumatic incident reduction facilitator.

Life is fluid and ever changing, with people growing and evolving. Life is not static, and achieving success is often fraught with adversity along the way. Our maturation from childhood innocents to the golden years is impacted by how we react to situations. Many people would attest that happiness and success are life goals and are also very personal experiences that contribute to a person's esteem and self-worth.

When the stars align and life is smoothly going as planned, we can be elated and calmly appreciate the simplicity of life. Imagine being at the top of your game, having a career, a loving family, kick-ass friends, and the financial freedom that many others envy. And then it suddenly changes. Trauma is the unwanted guest that comes to the party, runs amok, drinks all the booze—while lying about how they lost their invitation, thought they were never invited— and unapologetically leaves after stealing a party gift. When the event is over, you are left to clean up the mess, which can become overwhelming. You find things broken, your other guests are left trying to comprehend what happened, and even your dog is shaking its head in confusion. Trauma is merciless and often life altering.

Life has a way of creating the world you need. I'm a true believer that I was given the tools, even in my youth, to find the career I have today. What doesn't break you will only make you stronger. I remember being young, hearing this cliché statement, and thinking that wasn't going to be me. I was going to make myself unbreakable. I took my anger and found outlets in sports and recreation to manage my pain. I was determined to overcome my family inadequacies and become more than I was ever expected to be. Soccer became my therapy for my anger, and music healed my soul. I developed a determined mindset, particularly on a soccer field. And when I became overwhelmed, I found my voice as a singer in order to sooth the angst I felt when I became flooded with memories of the abuse. The trauma I endured and survived became a necessary part of my story, and I discovered the field of therapeutic recreation.

Trauma disrupts your peace of mind, your relationship with your-self, and your relationship with your loved ones, but it can also have lasting triggers that impede on how you continue living. The lasting impact of an experience is individual, and the consequences of a traumatic event can leave scars both visible and invisible. A car accident that causes a spinal cord injury, a fall off the playground equipment that causes a brain bleed, a natural disaster or global pandemic, any type of abuse or neglect, the onset of dementia, or even the death of a pet or loved one can affect the physical, emotional, cognitive, social, or spiritual well-being of a person. Trauma does not discriminate, nor is it concerned with the degree of its impacts. Trauma hurts and can rob a person of his or her happiness. One of the most relevant concerns is overcoming or coping with the nightmares and flashbacks associated with the event, which is called post-traumatic stress disorder (PTSD).

A car accident is an unfortunate but not uncommon event that can happen to a person in a lifetime. Let's say you acquire a life-altering spinal cord injury that requires surgery, rehabilitation, plastic surgery, weeks in the hospital, and months of recovery at home. The financial impact is huge. You have lost work and accrued more financial debt, and insurance is running out. The extended family is trying to help, but they can't experience everything you're going through. You may never walk again! Trauma changed your life without permission, and now you must cope with this new uncertainty, and you feel depressed. The idea of getting in a car causes an immediate panic attack, which is just the tip of the emotional iceberg of the long-term effects on your wellbeing, and now you're scheduled to meet the hospital recreation therapist. What is recreation therapy?

"*Recreational* **therapy,** *also known as* **therapeutic recreation,** *is a systematic process that utilizes* **recreation** *and other activity-based interventions to address the assessed needs of individuals with illnesses and/or disabling conditions, as a means to psychological and physical health, recovery and well-being.*" NCTRC website (insert proper city)

A recreation therapist is part of a person's rehabilitation program and can be an integral part of healing. We create custom individual programs and/or group programs based on the histories and assessments designed for your care. We can be employed in hospitals, community centers, nursing care programs, child protection agencies, and in private practice. We set measurable and achievable goals to alleviate or re-mediate your wellbeing, and we use carefully articulated care plans that encourage you to use recreation and leisure pursuits to heal. We get you to have fun and embrace your new lifestyle with activities of your choosing.

If a person living with an acquired spinal cord injury used to be an active hockey player, a recreation therapist might enroll that person in a leisure education class and introduce the game sledge hockey. That same individual may be suffering from post traumatic stress dis-order (PTSD) and might require traumatic incident reduction (TIR) to alleviate triggers, and that might be followed up with self-esteem and assertiveness training.

The recreation therapist will adapt and change the program as the individual's needs improve or require modification. We will also encourage the individual to achieve new successes by learning other activities, such as art, music, nature, games, and/or sports. We can create personal assessments and activity analysis to accommodate individual needs and modify accordingly. We can use community resources, including high intensity activities like rock climbing and lower intensity leisure experiences like walks or animal therapy. We are versed in the patterns of activities and in the psychology of the progression of well-being and health. We love the challenge of creating specific programs that help our clients overcome barriers in their own lives. We love teaching people that trauma does not have control and is **not** a life sentence. We will teach you how to play again!

Yoga: Healing Comes from Within

by Devanni Peters

When you look at trauma healing, yoga is a practice you do not want to overlook. It's a powerful practice that shifts the energy for healing. Yoga is not just a physical practice for the fit and flexible person; yoga is for everyone. The intention of yoga is to get you out of your pain and misery and bring you back into balance: the natural state of health and well-being. It is a true path to self-discovery.

I remember my first yoga class. Not having any idea what to expect, it was a bit intimidating. The once brightly lit workout room had now been transformed into a much calmer, softer space. The lights were dimmed, soft music played, and candles were gently flickering. I found a spot for my yoga mat and sat quietly, patiently waiting for the class to begin. The instructor guided us in a series of poses as we tried our best to follow. We were encouraged to breathe deeply, stay focused, and listen to our bodies. Everyone was at different levels, had different bodies, and had different issues. Staying within our limits was important. Yoga was not about competition or how we performed in the poses.

The class ended in Savasana (corpse pose), where we lay on our backs, covered ourselves with blankets, closed our eyes, and just lay still for a few minutes. As the mind and body relax, the breath and the brain slow down, and the blood pressure drops. This is a time for integration to calm the nervous system and listen to intuition.

After months of attending regular yoga classes, I became more flexible and stronger in my body, but I also felt a sense of calm that kept me coming back. The more I practiced, the more I began to realize that there was more to this than just a physical workout that challenged and transformed my body.

Nothing in the outside world can make you happy if you are not happy within yourself. Yoga is a practice of turning your attention inward, away from worldly distractions, so that you can hear the messages from within. When you do the yoga postures, you are not only rewarded with health, strength, and confidence, but you are also using your body as a vehicle to recognize blockages. Any unresolved issues you have—whether it's past trauma, unforgiveness, or anything that still triggers you—gets stored in your body, creating tension. If these issues are not dealt with fully, they will keep coming back to you as pain, irritation, and even disease.

Energy wants to move through you without restrictions. When you hold on to your past, it affects the flow of energy. Imagine your body as a tube. If all of your emotions and experiences are allowed to be expressed fully, they will stream in, through, and out of the tube in a constant flow, making it a powerful channel for new and rewarding experiences to come in. But if you have an experience where uncomfortable sensations come up and you choose to ignore or resist the feelings, they get stuck in the tube and can't move through, creating a block. This restricts the tube, not allowing for new experiences and expressions to come in. As a result, it keeps you stuck in the old patterns that aren't working.

Healing begins by speaking your truth, admitting to yourself what has happened and how it is affecting you in everyday life. To break free from the past, you have to step out of your comfort zone and transform. Without humility and vulnerability, nothing changes. Bring the feelings to the surface so you can face your fears. Pray, journal, or talk to someone you trust. When you become aware of your weaknesses and struggles, you will be inspired and empowered to change. It's only when you bring light to the situation that darkness disappears. You need awareness before change can happen.

It's important to find a safe way to connect with your body and feel. In yoga, you use inward focus and breath awareness to take you to the edge of the pose, get you out of our comfort zone, and get you into the body. You use the tension stored in the body for purification. As dis-comfort begins to build in the pose, you learn to feel and stay with the sensations and pulsations flooding through your body as you breathe deeply into it.

Keep your attention on the body and listen to your breath for instruction. Focusing on the breath will keep you safe in the pose. Anytime you are struggling with your breath, it is a sign you have gone too far, and you need to modify or back away from the pose. Never take yourself further than you are ready to go. It takes effort on your part, but not force. Find balance at the edge of the pose and, with the help of the breath, practice letting go, which allows for the release of pressure.

The breath is a powerful force to move energy. It will guide you to safely release what you have been holding on to. Connecting deeply with your breath connects you to your truth and prana. Prana is life force energy, or the Holy Spirit, that enters the body with the breath, directing the energy to heal.

Even though you cannot see energy, your intuition gives you clear signals through the sensations you feel flowing through your body. Notice your gut feelings or impulses and listen closely. Insight can come in the form of words, or it can just be knowing. Success in yoga is seeing the transformation that takes place in your everyday life and relation-ships. You will notice that the things that used to trigger you don't have the charge that they used to. It is moving through the tube and empowering you to have new and different experiences.

Once you begin to trust your inner being and return balance to your physical body, peace, harmony, and well-being begin to shine through you. If you have your health and well-being, you have everything. You can choose to live a long, healthy, and prosperous life, free and empowered!

Traumatic Incident Reduction

by Sandra Cooze

Traumatic incident reduction, TIR, is an amazing and, most of all, effective, <u>evidence-based</u> modality in the field of meta-psychology. The system of TIR was designed specifically for people who suffer from PTSD.

It works by releasing the emotional charge or trigger associated with a traumatic event. By releasing the emotional attachment to a trauma you had to experience, that trauma becomes just another part of your life story, no more or less significant than what you had to eat the day before.

The methodology of TIR is to walk the client through a traumatic incident repetitively through the means of powerful questioning. This method brings any triggers to the surface so they can be evaluated and released, until there is no emotional charge left. Once no emotions that are attached to the traumatic incident are left, the memory of the trauma will fade peacefully into the abyss and will just be a faint memory, like any other part of your life.

What I love most about this modality, which I practice myself, is how quickly it can bring results for my clients. It is astounding that if a person is truly ready to release their trauma, he or she can experience positive shifts after only two or three sessions, long before we even get into looking at the actual incident. The transformations I am blessed to witness are incredible. My clients report that they feel lighter. Some describe how they began to dress differently, were more outgoing, and felt less drawn to unhealthy habits that used to help suppress the pain. I see my clients become hopeful for a brighter future. I see them following their dreams, though they had no hope before starting with TIR

In TIR, the person guiding the client through the session is called "facilitator,' and the client is called "viewer," as he or she will be viewing his or her trauma in order to release it. Each session begins and ends with a session protocol. This session protocol is important because it determines whether the viewer is in the right condition and mindset for the session, e.g. alert, not hungry, not under the influence of any mind-altering substance, etc. Here is a rundown of how a session sequence works:

At the very beginning is the <u>Intake Interview</u>, which is when the facilitator will explain the concept of TIR to the viewer. In this session, the very first "items" that can be viewed will be determined and measured on a scale of how triggered the viewer feels at the mention of these items and how interested he or she is in looking at them. Items can be people, places, situations, or incidences. Emotions are also recorded but are generally connected to the different items and are rarely looked at separately.

The next session is focused on <u>Exploration</u> of one of the items on the list that the viewer chose. In this session, the viewer will talk about the item he or she chose. The facilitator will hold the space for the viewer to explore his or her trauma and take notes of any new item that comes to the surface during this exploration process.

In the following session, the viewer will begin <u>Unblocking</u> some of the trauma. This part usually takes several sessions. In an unblocking session, the facilitator will ask the viewer a series of twenty questions. Each question is specifically designed to help the viewer go deeper into the memories surrounding the chosen item and bring to the surface what has been missed in the <u>Exploration Session</u>. What is important here to note is that each question will be asked repeatedly, until nothing comes up for the viewer, in which case his or her mind will draw a blank. Then, and only then, will the facilitator move on to the next question. Unblocking is a very important step in TIR, as it allows the viewer to release many charges. What's so fascinating is that once issues that have been on the surface are released, items that have been completely forgotten will rise to the surface and into the consciousness of the viewer. I have heard so many times, "Oh, I just remembered something. That is so weird. I had completely forgotten about that!" This is a common phenomenon.

When you hold on to triggers, they block everything out that lies underneath. By releasing those charges, what was buried beneath will rise up next. This is how TIR works. By releasing layer by layer of traumatic memories and charges, you gradually get to the root cause, and once this root cause is released, there won't be any trauma from that particular incident left to hold you hostage.

Unblocking will release most of the charges associated with an item well before you get to the last part, which is the <u>Basic Traumatic Incident Reduction</u>.

In the final <u>TIR</u> session for the selected item, the viewer will choose an incident related to that item and will go through it over and over again until the charge is released. This sounds very intimidating and stressful, but don't be alarmed. The facilitator will make sure that the viewer is ready for this T.I.R. session. This means that by the time the viewer is ready to look at the traumatic incident, most of the triggers have already been released through <u>Exploration</u> and <u>Unblocking</u>. What is left is the incident itself. And by going through it over and over again, the charge or trigger can rise to the surface and be released.

One thing to note here is what can and most likely will happen right before the emotional release:

The body is trying to protect you from pain, no matter if it is physical, mental, or emotional. So, when you purposefully go into the trauma, the body will try and stop you. This can present itself as a sudden onset of nausea, rapid heart rate, cold sweats, heavy and fast breathing, or any other form of physical reaction. These reactions are normal and happen right before the release of the final trigger. As soon as the trigger is released, these sensations will stop.

I had a client who tended to throw up every time we "hit a nerve." This is nothing alarming. It actually meant that we were on the right track. You see, the body, in a way, tries to suppress the trauma and yet, at the same time, tries to release it. And for some, this presents itself as throwing up. But here is the thing: At the beginning of a basic TIR session, she had to throw up almost constantly, but half way through it just stopped and at the end even the nausea was gone. There was no need to throw up. There was no trigger or charge left. The trauma was just a part of her life story and didn't have any significance or weight. It was just gone. No more nausea or vomiting. Even when I asked about it in a following session, she did not have any connection to that incident any longer, and she even used the item name as her mantra. This was a ritual she started. She chanted the name of all of the items she had gradually released, because she had no emotional connection to them anymore. It was so wonderful witnessing her transformation.

I have had many clients who have felt nauseous even in the <u>Intake Interview</u>, when we talked about how TIR works. The thought of going into the trauma to release it can be terrifying, and the body reacts accordingly to protect. The very fact that my clients had such a reaction in the very first session shows how close to the surface the triggers already were and how ready they were to release them.

Once the TIR session for that item is complete and the viewer has released everything that was related to the item chosen, he or she will determine the next item and begin a new session sequence, starting with Exploration.

If you want to know more about TIR, I would begin by looking for a TIR facilitator in your area. Visit the website of the Traumatic Incident Reduction Association at www.tira.org, or reach out to me at www.riseaboveyourstory.com.

TIR can be facilitated in person or through video conferences.

Coaching

by Sandra Cooze

Coaching is an interesting profession. Before I decided to study the art and science of coaching at Ericson College in Vancouver, I thought that anyone could just call themselves a coach if they felt drawn to help people through life hurdles. But boy, was I ever wrong. The techniques that a certified coach can implement are incredible. By merely asking targeted questions and using specific visualization techniques, the coach can guide the client through the maze of her mind and find the solution that has been within her from the start. A coach does not tell her client what to do or how to do it; instead, the coach helps her to see that she already has the answers. Most of the time, the client was just too scared to go to that place of fulfillment.

Most people seek out a coach when they are feeling stuck. A coach can help a person find her way out of this "stuckness" and away from what holds her back.

The greatest power a coach has is understanding how to listen. When we listen to someone, we mostly listen to reply, to talk about ourselves or to patronize. But to truly listen without an agenda is a special skill that has to be learned. Coaches are trained to listen without an agenda. They learn to truly hear what you say and what you are not saying.

Let me tell you a little story. One night, our then six-year-old son came into our bedroom around midnight. This was unusual. Normally, he would just go to the bathroom and then straight back to bed. He didn't say anything while standing next to me, and then he just turned around and went to the bathroom and then back to sleep. Still, it was a bit strange.

The next day, he did not remember the incident, as I had expected. That evening, though, when my husband took him to bed, he suddenly erupted into a panic. He started to cry and scream hysterically that he did not want to go to sleep and dream about him dying again. So, he must have had a nightmare the night before about himself being dead. My husband could not calm him down, and our son called for me.

Seeing my son in such distress was heartbreaking. Normally, I would have held him and hoped that his fear would disappear and that he would calm down, but I would probably not have been able to shift his mindset. I would not have known what to do in that moment. Well, thanks to my coaching education, I was trained for situations like this one. When I held my son in my arms, I instinctively went into "coach position" and just listened. I heard him repeat, "I do not want to dream about dying anymore!" So I asked, "Well, what do you want to dream about?" That was the million-dollar question. That was the question that moved him out of his terrified mindset almost instantly. He said, "I want to dream about something fun." So I asked him to tell me about a time when he had fun, and he started talking about being at the playground the other day and the kids he had played with, and he laughed and was happy again. This happened in a matter of less than three minutes   after I took him into my arms. He went to sleep happily that night, hopefully dreaming about his time on the playground.

What happened here was that I was solely focusing my attention on him. Generally, we focus our attention to the problem and try to find a solution, focusing our attention within ourselves to find the answer. In this case, I did not focus on myself at all. I was just listening to my child and responding to what he was telling me.

The thing with listening is that, for the most part, we listen with an agenda. We listen to reply, we listen to give advice, or we listen to patronize. But we hardly ever listen just to listen. When you seek out a coach to help you through your trauma, you will find that the coach, for the most part, just listens and then asks very specific questions. This question may trigger you, but that is intentional. Only by observing what triggers us can we release it.

I love coaching my clients. Seeing how a simple question can transform the mindset of a person is so amazingly rewarding. Coaches choose their field based on their own experiences or passions. No two coaches are alike.

> "As coaches, we create a safe space so our clients
> can explore their impossible dreams until
> they realize that they are not impossible at all."
>
> —Sandra Cooze

Crystals

by Sandra Cooze

Crystals are a truly fascinating subject. Did you know that you have a quartz crystal in virtually any electronic device you own? You have one in your phone, tablet, computer, microwave, TV, and so on and so forth.

Many crystals, aside from quartz, are used as energy conductors in all kinds of technical devices.

Crystals emit and absorb energy. I have witnessed this phenomenon in my clients' and my own bracelets. When crystals absorb your energy and hold on to it, the energy in between the crystal beads will increase, sometimes to the point that your bracelet or necklace will explode. I had a couple clients who reported this issue. As annoying as it may be, it is also truly fascinating. Energy takes up space and expands, even if we can not see it. Energy can build up so much pressure that it breaks a beaded bracelet on a metal wire, or even strong, sterling silver chain links. Can you imagine? I find that remarkable!

But let's take a look at a more scientific view of how incredible crystals truly are:

German scientists have discovered that our cells emit low-grade electromagnetic fields called biophotons. These biophotons help cells to communicate with each other. (More information about this subject can be found in the book Biophotonen: Das Licht in unseren Zellen (translation: Biophotons: The Light in our Cells) by Marco Bischof.

Further studies have shown that electromagnetic radiation from crystals affect these biophotons. It was discovered that energy from the crystals changed patterns in the brain when the crystals were placed near or on the body. (More information about this subject can be found in the research papers of the Institut für kinesiologische Pädiatrie ([Translation: Institute for kinesiological Pediatrics], Dr. Kühl, Reutlingen).

Michael Gienger, a worldwide expert on crystal healing, who has studied crystals for over thirty years, said "[Crystals] emit measurable frequencies of radiation in the range of infrared and ultraviolet, as well as of visible light. And although radiation from crystals is of a low intensity, because of its regularity and duration it does have great effect! For comparison, imagine a vibrating guitar string, which can barely be heard in a room, but that sounds beautifully loud through the medium of the guitar's wooden body. Analogously, the weak radiation of a crystal may at times cause a strong reaction in our organism."

I am so happy that I can share some scientific research with you that proves that crystals and stones are more than just pretty rocks.

Working with crystals falls into the same category as practicing or receiving Reiki or performing yoga and other holistic practices. You don't have to believe that they work, but you should, at the very least, give them the benefit of the doubt. Be open to exploring the possibility that they may work as intended.

Crystals have been used throughout the ages and are cherished in every culture. Just as someone who works with essential oils would say, "I have an oil for that!" I always say, "I have a crystal for that!" Now, just imagine if you combined the two and had a bracelet created specifically for your needs, with the right crystals and a list of the right essential oils!

There is an infinite number of different crystals out there, and each one is unique in shape, size, color, and energy nuance. The power of crystals and their amazing healing vibration has been known throughout the ages. Crystals have been used as jewelry, ground up in elixirs, or used as pigment. They have been used for their beauty, healing, and protection.

Let's imagine a person standing in front of you. This person has a health issue. From previous chapters, we have learned that everything is energy, and everything vibrates in a specific frequency nuance. A healthy person would vibrate differently than an unhealthy one. This is where the crystals come in. Choosing the crystal, or crystals, that are known to help with that specific ailment will help the body to adjust the frequency in that body part back to a healthy vibration. And that can help the person heal.

For trauma, there are many wonderful crystals out there that will help. But here it is important to note that different trauma may require different crystals. Some crystals that I would recommend for any kind of trauma are rose quartz, clear quartz, and tiger's eye. The rose quartz helps with love and self-love, and it helps you release what is weighing heavy on your heart and find yourself. The clear quartz will release negative energy and replace it with positive. Remember my healing story? The clear quartz was the first crystal I ever used, and I had incredible results with it. The tiger's eye will help you to stay grounded while you heal.

If you feel drawn to crystals and their healing energy and would like to wear them in jewelry, reach out to me, and I will design a bracelet specifically for you and your needs.

Reiki

by Sandra Cooze

When it comes to trauma healing, Reiki is a wonderful addition to any treatment plan you have. If you read the chapter "The Separation of Body and Soul," where I talk in detail about what happens to your body during and after an assault or rape, then you will remember that you separate yourself from your body and leave it to its own devices. Reiki can help you to reconnect to your body and, at the same time, release the physical and emotional pain.

As I have said before, everything is energy, and so pain is also rooted in energy. Reiki will help to release the energy that is stuck in the fibers of your body, caused by the traumatic event(s), and help you heal.

Whenever I give Reiki treatments, I can always tell when energy is emotional. This energy quite fascinatingly just slips out of my grasp each time I try to remove it. I call it elusive energy. The first time I noticed how energy was slipping away, I was giving a friend of mine a Reiki treatment. She had just beat breast cancer and had a clean bill of health, but she still felt as if something had remained. She felt a slight pressure in her chest.

First, I performed her treatment routinely, and then I went back to focus on her chest area. She was right. There was some energy stuck. It did feel like sticky tar, which told me that it had already become stagnant and was not too far from causing discomfort. So I started working on removing the energy. To my surprise, as I was working on it, the energy suddenly vanished. At first, I was stunned because I knew that the energy could not just have jumped out of the body, especially when it felt so stiff and thick. So I kept working around her chest area, and then I "found" the energy again. It had moved a bit to the side of her body. So I started working on it again, and again it slipped away.

As I was working on her chest, I had not sensed any energy that would indicate inflammation or infection, so I knew the cancer had not returned. The rather mobile energy did make me curious, though. So I asked my friend if she felt as if something was still there, and she said yes. My reply to her was that I did not sense anything malicious energetically. I further asked her whether she was afraid to believe that the cancer was truly gone, and she said yes. Then I realized that the sticky and elusive energy was her fear of letting the emotional toll of the cancer go. I talked to her about my theory, and she began to calm down, which also calmed the energy down enough for me to remove it. Once I was done, she felt as if a heaviness had been lifted off of her chest. This was in 2018, and the cancer has not returned.

The next significant encounter I had with elusive energy was with a long-term client of mine. She had suffered a lot of loss in her family over the previous six months and was just about to bury another cousin. She had pain in her lower back. Aside from other health issues, this pain was rather new. As I was working on her back, the energy started to slip out of my fingers and move away. From past experiences, I knew that this meant an emotional blockage rather than an actual health issue. So I talked to her about my theory of elusive energy, which helped her to open up about her emotional pain from losing so many family members so soon and her guilt for not feeling able to go and see her dead cousin before the burial. As she was talking, the energy started to flow out of her back. When she left after her session, she said that she already felt 100 percent better. The pain in her lower back was completely gone.

With emotional blockages, the energy can be anywhere in the body. When a person is not ready to let go of emotional pain, he or she will try to hold on to the energy.

Elusive energy is an interesting phenomenon, as it shows how much control you actually have over energy and your emotions. You can create energetic blockages without knowing it. You may feel stiffness or a sudden onset of pain in different areas that just won't go away. And if you don't know anything about your own ability to create pain, you keep suffering for years. Yet once you are ready to let go, no matter if it is knowingly or unknowingly, the pain will gradually subside as the energy shifts and leaves your body.

With Reiki, we have the advantage because we can help the energy leave once a person is ready to let it go. This is why I highly recommend Reiki as part of your healing regime. If you have a Reiki practitioner you regularly see, talk to them about elusive energy.

The Next Step in Your Healing Journey

Now that you have made it to the end of my book, you are probably thinking, *And now what?* Well, I do hope, of course, that I gave you enough insight and encouragement to begin your journey to Your Self by healing the trauma that you have undoubtedly been holding on to for way too long.

On the other hand, if you are feeling empowered to heal your trauma but are not quite sure where to start, or if you feel overwhelmed by the thought of going on this journey on your own, I would love for you to reach out to me. Together, we can design the perfect action plan for your healing journey based on your hopes, dreams, beliefs, and intentions.

My process begins with a free consultation. We will dive deep into your situation and explore your past, your present, what you wish to achieve by working with me, and how I can help you to get there.

To book your consultation, please visit my website, www.riseaboveyourstory.com, and look for a button that says "book your free consultation today." This will lead you to my online calendar, where you can pick a day and time to connect with me via a Zoom call.

And while you are on my website, why don't you browse through my blog, check out the different programs I offer, or subscribe to my email list so you can stay up to date with new articles and courses, and of course to get notified when the next book in the Journey to Your Self Series is coming out. If you loved what I wrote about my jewelry, I invite you to check it out in my shop, which is also located on my website.

If you have a question about trauma healing that you would like answered, send me a message at sandra@riseaboveyourstory.com, or get in touch with me on Facebook, @riseaboveyourstory, or LinkedIn, @sandracooze. I would also like to invite you to subscribe to my YouTube channel @SandraCoozeUnfiltered, where you will find short videos with subjects surrounding different aspects of trauma healing and spiritual development.

Afterword

I hope you enjoyed this book and found value in the past chapters.

Most of my clients are women, usually wives and mothers who seek help to heal their unresolved past trauma, transform their relationship with their partner, children, family and friends, or seek ways to empower themselves to reach their full potential.

The beauty is that everything we strive to be is already within us. If we want to be strong and resilient, we already have that strength and resilience within us, buried underneath all of the fear that has accumulated over the years and taken hold of our bodies, minds, and spirits. If we want to be courageous and go for what we want without second-guessing everything, we already have that courage within ourselves, buried underneath all of the self-doubt that has built up over the years due to past experiences.

Envision yourself as the ballerina of an animated jewelry box. Inside this musical jewelry box is a set of gears and springs that make the ballerina dance once it is wound up. If a gear is out of alignment, the ballerina won't be able to dance, as the musical jewelry box seems to be broken. Most people would just throw this musical box away and buy a new one, but ultimately, the new one will also stop working simply because the issue the first one had will reappear in the new one. But rather than try to figure out what's wrong and try to fix it—because it seems way too intimidating, too hard to handle, or like way too much work—they discard this one, as well. They may buy a new one or just give up and live without a musical jewelry box to bring them joy.

If you would look at those misaligned gears as parts of yourself that are misaligned, it could look something like this: One gear could be self-doubt. Another gear could be fear of failure. Another gear could be self-preservation. Each of these gears is out of alignment. But once you have overcome your fears, your self-doubt, or your need to protect and control every aspect of your life and everyone in it, the gears will automatically move into place, and the ballerina will dance.

So, you see, the trauma you had to experience did not break you. It just temporarily misaligned parts of you. All you need to do is take the first step and decide that you will take it upon yourself to fix what is misaligned within the mechanism of that musical jewelry box.

Trauma healing can be a wonderful experience. It all depends on your mindset. If you are ready to leave the past behind, you will gladly lean into the pain and ultimately discover transformation. You will see yourself change rapidly. But when you are not ready, when you resent yourself, your life, the incident, and the people involved and hold on to your anger and your pain, your healing journey can become extremely painful.

If you find that you resent the thought of letting go of your trauma, ask yourself, "What am I afraid of?" and then follow that thought to its root. When you resent something, it is always out of fear. And fear is an illusion that is created by your mind to protect you from perceived danger, pain, or other negative experiences. Once you understand the root of your fear, it loses its power over you, and you can let it go.

With that, I am going to end my book. I wish you all the best in your healing journey. Rise Above Your Story and Thrive!

But before I let you go; I would like to draw your attention to the very last paragraph of my acknowledgement:

"I am giving a shout out to all those individuals who let me down, bullied, threatened, manipulated, humiliated, and abused me. It is because of your violation of my body, mind, and spirit that I discovered a strength and resilience I never knew I had. You instilled a darkness within me that helped me discover my light. Let it be known far and wide: I chose to thrive not despite what you did, but because of it."

With gratitude,
Sandra Cooze

Works-in-Progress

Journey to Your Self
How to Unbecome Who You were Taught to Be

In the second book of this trilogy, I will take you on a journey through the mysteries of limiting beliefs, self-sabotage, unconscious fears, coping mechanisms, and how generational and ancestral trauma can greatly influence your healing journey. I will, among other things, focus on setting healthy boundaries, touching on narcissistic relationships and how to finally break free, and of course I again will provide you with wonderful journaling techniques, unique exercises, leave room for notes and much more, to help you advance in your healing journey.

Journey to Your Self
How to Become Your True Self

This last book of my transformational trilogy is focused on creating the life that you have always wanted. Gone are all the deep traumas, tormenting triggers, and limiting beliefs. I will teach you to stand in your power, be confident in any situation, attract what you want into your life, and much more. I will also teach you my process of shifting into flow and how that method can help you live a happy and fulfilled life every day. You will learn how to bring into your life what you desire by manifesting successfully, how to adjust your surroundings to harbor only the highest vibrational energy, and so much more.

Trauma Reiki

Companion Book of the Trauma Reiki Certification Course

Trauma energy has a unique signature. Over the past few years, I have incorporated Reiki more and more into my trauma healing practice and what it taught me in the process is mind-blowing. Trauma Reiki will enrich your life and the life of your patients and clients immensely. I will teach you everything you need to know about trauma, how it works in the body, and what key role energy plays. I will teach you my method of using energy work to release even the toughest trigger, and with that help your clients heal in an even more profound way. I will show you how you can use Trauma Reiki as a stand-alone practice, or how to incorporate it into your therapy, counseling, or coaching sessions.

Death Taught Me How to Live
(Transformational Fiction)

Amanda Stanton is a modern-day debutante from one of the wealthiest families in north America. The night before her wedding to Kendrick McKenzie, handsome son of a hotel tycoon, she walks in on him and his former fiancée.

Furious and heartbroken she calls off the wedding and finds herself alone on a tropical island on what should have been her honeymoon.

As she walks along the beach one beautiful morning, she notices something slightly resembling a huge, round, black glass mirror hovering a few feet above the ground. Not knowing whether she has completely lost her mind, or if she is simply seeing a reflection of something from the water, she curiously walks closer only to see herself dressed like Xena jump out of that mirror, telling Amanda, that it is about time she shows up, grabbing her hand, and pulling her into the portal to a destination that will change her life forever.

<u>Author's Note:</u> I had this story in my head for years, and I am so excited to finally have picked up my pen and being on my journey of bringing it to life. My intention with this book series is to bring what I have taught you in my 'Journey to Your Self' trilogy into a format that will guide you through the process of healing and transformation through the eyes of the main characters. I do hope you will enjoy reading it just as much as I am enjoying writing it.

Courses-In-Progress

Trauma Reiki

Trauma Reiki is a certification course for Reiki practitioners who are ready to take their healing practice to the next level. You will learn to understand the role energy plays in trauma, how it is stored in our body, how to spot it, and how to successfully release it. You will learn how to use Trauma Reiki in emergency situations to release panic-, and PTSD attacks in a matter of minutes, successfully bringing a person back into balance. You will understand trauma, as well as energy from a whole new perspective. The prerequisite for this course is Reiki Level I or higher. At the end of this course, you will be certified in Trauma Reiki and will receive a certificate that states 'Trauma Informed Reiki Practitioner'.

Intimacy After Trauma

The intimate moments with your partner are the most treasured times. A hug, a kiss on the forehead, snuggling, or holding hands while watching TV. All these moments are treasures.

Being sexually intimate should be just as magical, and yet so many couples struggle when it comes to sex and being physically intimate.

Sex is one of those things almost everyone loves doing but feels terribly uncomfortable talking about.

However, not being able to openly talk about sex is not the only, or biggest issue. Trauma is. I have been working with many women who were sexually assaulted, raped, or body shamed and as a result of that experienced triggers whenever they were trying to be intimate with their loving partner.

Sexual trauma can cause so many issues. Not only does it cause sex to become a triggering subject, but it can wreak havoc on your relationship. It is often frustrating for both partners for different reasons. And if not addressed, can become the reason why relationships break apart.

In this course I will teach you how you can help your partner, or work together as a couple, to overcome intimacy issues and release trauma for good.

Boundary Boot Camp

Boundaries are the greatest act of self-love. In this course I will teach you how to set healthy boundaries with yourself and others, how to stand your ground when someone willfully ignores your boundaries, and how to stand in your power, and be confident in your decisions.

Acknowledgments

Writing a book takes time and lots of hours in silent contemplation; at least for me. Creativity is also something I can't just switch on or off. Therefore, I would love to thank my husband, Jim, for keeping our son Cedric occupied whenever my creative juices decided to flow. I could not have written this book without your support. No matter if it was a shoulder I needed to cry on or when I forgot how late it was and wrote way past dinner time. I could always count on you to hold down the fort and give me the time and space I needed to write and create. I love you!

There are many wonderful people who have positively impacted my life and given me room to grow into the person I have always been meant to become. And so, I would like to thank everyone who lifted me up when I was down and encouraged me when I was ready to throw in the towel. In this regard, I would like to extend a special and heartfelt thank you to my mother Annemarie Henning, my sister Andrea Fraeger, and Pati, my aunt and godmother Gisela Rogge.

Beth (Lala) Potrykus, Don Hauser, and Lana Chandler. You laughed with me, you cried with me, you lifted me up when I was down and grounded me when I needed it the most. You pushed me forward or pulled me back whenever I got lost within myself. I am so grateful to have each and every one of you in my life. You saw the light in me long before I ever could.

I would like to offer my special thanks to my friend Janice Peter-son for the beautiful drawings of various nutshells she designed for this book. And to my friend Saskia Willis for her incredible patience over the years while taking hundreds of pictures of me until I finally spotted one that I liked (oh boy). A big thank you to Saskia, as well, for the pictures you took of me modeling the Mudra hand positions for this book.

Bridget Klingbeil, Laurie Dulac, and Angelica Rivers, thank you so much for allowing me to share parts of your stories in my book. You transformed right in front of my eyes. As your coach I could not have asked for anything more.

I would like to express my gratitude to Melissa Tar, Devanni Peters, and Graham Nicholls for sharing parts of their stories as well as their passion and purpose in my book. Your unique modalities and approaches to trauma healing will open the doors for so many survivors who feel lost in their past.

My deepest heartfelt appreciation goes out to my photographer Brigitte Bourgoin. You captured me in a light I had never seen before. I have never felt pretty, let alone beautiful, due to the extreme bullying I endured growing up. But you showed me how wrong that perception was. You captured a side of me that I only ever dared to dream of. Thank you so much for that!

I would also like to thank my editor, Stephanie Renaud for her excellent work and support in publishing Journey to Your Self–How to Heal from Trauma.

Reflecting on my decision to write Journey to Your Self, the driving force was my story of abuse and what I had learned about myself and the concept of trauma while focusing on my own transformation. Therefore, I am ending my acknowledgment with a rather unusual group of people.

I am giving a shout out to all those individuals who let me down, bullied, threatened, manipulated, humiliated, and abused me. It is because of your violation of my body, mind, and spirit that I discovered a strength and resilience I never knew I had. You instilled a darkness within me that helped me discover my light. Let it be known far and wide: I chose to thrive not despite what you did, but because of it.

www.ingramcontent.com/pod-product-compliance
Lightning Source LLC
Chambersburg PA
CBHW011931050726
47590CB00011B/3238